# The Art of Letting Go

# The Art of Letting Go

Overcoming Ego and Letting Go

*Evangeline Brooks*

*Mindful Pages*

Published in 2024

ISBN: 9789358813449 (PB)
ISBN: 9789358814279 (eBook)

*Published by*

Mindful Pages
Imprint of Alpha Editions LLC
312 W. 2nd St #1834
Casper, WY 82601, USA

# Contents

# *Chapter 1: Understanding Attachment and Ego the ego*

In our quest for happiness and peace, we often encounter two formidable forces that subtly shape our lives: attachment and ego. Understanding these concepts is an intellectual exercise and a vital step towards self-awareness and spiritual growth. This chapter serves as our starting point, a deep dive into the intricacies of attachment and ego and how they intertwine to influence our thoughts, emotions, and behaviours.

We begin with attachment – a term that evokes various images and meanings. In its broadest sense, attachment is our emotional bond to people, things, ideas, and even past experiences. While some attachments can be healthy and nurturing, others might lead us into cycles of dependency, fear, and dissatisfaction.

The Nature of Attachment: Understanding its various forms, from material possessions and relationships to beliefs and past experiences.

The Psychology of Attachment: How attachment develops, its roots in childhood, and its impact on adult life.

Attachment's Impact on Well-being: Examining how unhealthy attachments can lead to emotional turbulence and hinder personal growth.

## Ego: The Self Construct

Next, we turn our attention to the ego. Often misunderstood, the ego is more than just arrogance or self-importance. It is the sense of 'I' or 'self' that perceives and interacts with the world around us. The ego is a complex construct, playing a crucial role in our identity and survival, but it can also be a source of suffering and illusion.

## Defining the Ego

Ego and Identity: How our ego shapes our perception of self and the world.

The Dual Nature of Ego: Understanding how the ego can be both a tool for survival and a barrier to proper understanding and peace.

The Interplay of Attachment and Ego

Finally, we'll explore the dynamic interplay between attachment and ego. These two forces often work hand-in-hand, with our ego reinforcing our attachments and our attachments feeding our ego. This cycle can be a significant obstacle to personal growth and spiritual enlightenment.

**Understanding the Connection**

The Cycle of Desire and Dissatisfaction: Exploring how ego-driven attachments lead to a never-ending cycle of desire and disappointment.

Breaking the Cycle: Introducing concepts and practices that will help us start the journey of releasing these bonds.

As we navigate this chapter, I encourage you to reflect on your experiences with attachment and ego. By understanding these fundamental aspects of our nature, we set the stage for a deeper exploration into the art of letting go. This journey is about more than shedding unnecessary baggage; it's about discovering a lighter, more authentic, and more joyful way of living.

# Define Attachment and Ego in Spiritual and Psychological Contexts

In the realms of spirituality and psychology, the concepts of attachment and ego occupy central roles, but their interpretations and implications differ significantly between these disciplines. This article aims to delve into these differences, offering a comprehensive understanding of how attachment and ego are perceived and defined in both spiritual and psychological contexts.

**Attachment in Psychological Context**

In psychological terms, attachment is rooted in the theories of John Bowlby and Mary Ainsworth, who pioneered attachment theory in the mid-20th century. This theory posits that early relationships, particularly with primary caregivers, significantly influence an individual's emotional and relational development.

*Early Development and Types of Attachment:* According to Bowlby, the nature of a child's attachment to their caregivers forms the basis for future emotional and social outcomes. Secure attachment, where caregivers provide consistent and responsive care, promotes healthy emotional development. In contrast, insecure attachments, characterized by neglect or inconsistency, can result in emotional and relational difficulties.

*Impact on Adult Relationships:* The echoes of these early attachment styles are evident in adult relationships. Psychologists have linked secure attachment styles to healthier, more satisfying relationships. In contrast, insecure attachment styles can lead to a range of issues, from clinginess and dependency to emotional detachment and fear of intimacy.

*Attachment as a Lifelong Influence:* Psychologists view attachment not as a static trait but as a dynamic process that can evolve with experiences and relationships throughout one's life. Therapy and personal growth can alter attachment styles, moving from insecure to more secure attachment patterns.

## Attachment in Spiritual Context

In spiritual discourse, attachment takes on a broader, more existential meaning. It is often viewed as a source of suffering and a barrier to enlightenment or spiritual freedom.

*Buddhism and the Concept of Attachment:* Attachment (Upādāna) is a fundamental cause of suffering (Dukkha). This encompasses attachment to physical objects, concepts, identities, and desires. The Buddha taught that attachment arises from ignorance of the true nature of reality, leading to craving and clinging and consequently to a cycle of rebirth and suffering (Samsara).

*Attachment in Other Spiritual Traditions:* Similarly, in Hinduism, attachment (Raga) is seen as a bond to the material world that hinders spiritual liberation (Moksha). In Christian mysticism, attachment to worldly desires is viewed as a distraction from the path to spiritual union with God.

*The Spiritual Path of Detachment:* In these traditions, the path to spiritual liberation involves cultivating detachment or non-attachment. This is not a call to indifference or a lack of love but rather an encouragement to experience life fully without being enslaved by desires and fears.

## Ego in Psychological Context

In psychology, particularly in psychoanalytic theory developed by Sigmund Freud, the ego is part of a three-part structure of the mind, alongside the id and the superego.

*The Ego as a Mediator:* Freud described the ego as the rational part of the mind that mediates between the id's primal desires and the superego's moralistic demands. It's responsible for realistic planning, problem-solving, and defense mechanisms that help individuals cope with reality.

*Ego Development and Health:* A healthy ego is essential for effective functioning and psychological well-being. It's associated with self-awareness, self-esteem, and navigating complex social and emotional landscapes.

*Ego in Modern Psychology:* Contemporary psychology often uses the term 'ego' to refer more broadly to the sense of self or identity. A strong sense of self is crucial for psychological health, but excessive self-focus or egocentrism can lead to difficulties in relationships and emotional well-being.

## Ego in Spiritual Context

In spiritual contexts, particularly in Eastern philosophies, the ego is often seen as an illusionary sense of self distinct from one's true nature.

*Buddhism and the Non-Self:* In Buddhism, the concept of Anatta (no-self) suggests that the ego, or the sense of a separate self, is an illusion. True enlightenment involves realizing this and experiencing the interconnectedness of all beings.

*Hinduism and the Atman:* While the ego (Ahamkara) is recognized as part of the mind, it is seen as distinct from the true self (Atman). The Atman is eternal and unchanging, whereas the ego is transient and a source of illusion (Maya).

*Ego in Western Spirituality:* In Western spirituality, especially in mystical traditions, the ego is often seen as a barrier to experiencing a union with the divine. The spiritual journey involves transcending the ego to achieve a more profound, more authentic reality experience.

While psychology and spirituality offer different lenses to view attachment and ego, both disciplines agree on their significant impact on human experience. Psychology approaches these concepts with a focus on development, behaviour, and well-being, while spirituality views them as crucial elements in

# Human Nature

Humans, by nature, are complex beings driven by various psychological and emotional mechanisms. Among these are the tendencies towards material attachments, ego-driven behaviours, and holding grudges. Each aspect plays a significant role in shaping our experiences, interactions, and overall well-being. This article explores these tendencies, understanding their roots, implications, and the pathways they open or close in our lives.

## Material Attachments: The Quest for Possessions

Material attachment refers to the tendency to ascribe significant value to physical objects and possessions. This behaviour is deeply rooted in the human psyche, often driven by cultural, psychological, and evolutionary factors.

*Psychological and Cultural Factors:* From a psychological standpoint, possessions can become extensions of the self, representing one's identity, status, and achievements. Culturally, consumerism and materialism often promote the idea that happiness and success are tied to what one owns. This societal pressure can intensify the pursuit of material wealth and possessions.

*Evolutionary Perspective:* Evolutionarily, the desire to accumulate resources can be traced back to survival instincts. Our ancestors who were successful in resource accumulation were more likely to survive and reproduce, passing down these traits.

*The Downside of Material Attachment:* While material possessions are necessary for comfort and survival, excessive attachment can lead to perpetual desire and dissatisfaction. It can also foster a comparative mindset, where one's worth and happiness are constantly measured against others' possessions.

## Ego-Driven Behaviours: The Self in Focus

Ego-driven behaviours are actions influenced by an inflated sense of self-importance and a preoccupation with one's status and image. In this context, the ego is the part of the self-concerned with identity and self-presentation.

*Understanding the Ego:* In psychological terms, the ego is a necessary component of the human psyche, helping in self-organization and navigation of social worlds. However, when the ego becomes overinflated, it can lead to narcissistic traits, a need for constant validation, and conflict with others.

*Societal and Environmental Influences:* Ego-driven behaviours are often exacerbated by societal values emphasising competition, success, and personal achievement. Social media and contemporary culture often reward self-promotion and competition, which can further amplify these traits.

*The Impact of Ego:* An unchecked ego can damage relationships, lead to unrealistic expectations of oneself and others, and result in a lack of empathy and understanding. It can hinder personal growth and direct to a life driven by external validation rather than inner fulfilment.

## Holding Grudges: The Weight of Unforgiveness

Holding grudges is a psychological state where one harbours ongoing feelings of resentment or anger towards someone who has wronged them. While a natural response to perceived injustice, this tendency can have profound implications on emotional and physical health.

*Psychological Roots:* Grudges often stem from a violation of personal values or betrayal. They can be a defence mechanism to protect oneself from further emotional hurt. However, holding onto these negative emotions can lead to a state of chronic stress and emotional turmoil.

*Impact on Health and Relationships:* Research has shown that holding grudges can increase the risk of heart disease, mental health issues, and diminish overall life satisfaction. It also affects relationships, leading to mistrust and a communication breakdown.

*Letting Go and Forgiveness:* Letting go of grudges and moving towards forgiveness is often more beneficial to the individual holding the grudge than the one who wronged them. Forgiveness is not about condoning hurtful actions but about freeing oneself from the burden of resentment.

## Conclusions: Breaking Free from Destructive Tendencies

Understanding and acknowledging these human tendencies is the first step towards managing them. By recognizing the reasons behind our material attachments, ego-driven behaviours, and propensity to hold grudges, we can start to address these issues constructively.

*Finding Balance in Materialism:* It involves balancing enjoying material possessions and not letting them define one's happiness and self-worth. Mindfulness and gratitude practices can shift focus from what one lacks to what one has, fostering a sense of contentment.

*Ego Management:* For ego-driven behaviours, self-awareness and empathy are essential. Engaging in self-reflection, seeking feedback from others, and focusing on collaborative successes rather than individual accolades can help keep the ego in check.

*The Power of Forgiveness:* Regarding holding grudges, embracing forgiveness and understanding can lead to emotional liberation and improved well-being. Therapy, meditation, and open communication can assist in this process.

In conclusion, while material attachments, ego-driven behaviours, and holding grudges are ingrained human tendencies, they are not unchangeable. Through awareness, reflection, and intentional action, individuals can navigate these aspects of the human experience in a way that promotes personal growth, healthier relationships, and a more fulfilling life.

# Letting Go: A Transformative Spiritual Practice

The concept of 'letting go' has been a cornerstone in various spiritual traditions and philosophies for centuries. It is a practice that encompasses a broad range of meanings, from releasing physical possessions to detaching from thoughts and emotions. At its core, letting go is a transformative process that involves shedding the layers of attachment, fear, and ego that inhibit spiritual growth and personal freedom. This article aims to unpack this profound and often misunderstood concept, exploring its various dimensions and the pathways it opens for profound spiritual transformation.

## The Essence of Letting Go

To understand the essence of letting go, exploring what it truly entails is essential. Letting go is often misconceived as giving up or losing something valuable. However, in a spiritual context, it represents a conscious choice to release control and attachment to outcomes, possessions, and even identities. This release is not about loss but about gaining freedom, peace, and a deeper connection with the self and the world.

## Historical and Cultural Perspectives

Historically, letting go is deeply embedded in Eastern spiritual traditions. In Buddhism, letting go is linked to non-attachment, a fundamental principle to achieve enlightenment. The Buddha taught that attachment leads to suffering, and that liberation comes from releasing these attachments. Similarly, Hindu scriptures speak of Moksha, or liberation, achieved by letting go of the ego and realizing the true Self.

In Western spiritual traditions, letting go is often connected with surrender and trust in a higher power. Christian mystics, for example, spoke of 'dying to self' or letting go of one's ego and desires to experience union with God. This theme is also present in Islamic Sufism, where letting go is part of the journey towards divine love and surrender.

## Psychological Dimensions of Letting Go

From a psychological perspective, letting go involves releasing the mental and emotional grips that past experiences, fears, and expectations have on us. This includes letting go of grudges, resentments, and past hurts, which can be transformative for emotional well-being. Modern psychology recognizes the benefits of this practice, noting its role in reducing anxiety stress, and improving relationships.

## Material Letting Go

One of the most tangible forms of letting go is the release of material possessions and the detachment from physical objects. In a world increasingly driven by consumerism, this aspect of letting go challenges the notion that happiness and success are defined by what we own. This practice isn't about living with nothing but recognizing that true contentment comes from within, not external possessions.

## Emotional and Mental Release

Perhaps more challenging than releasing physical possessions is letting go of emotions and thoughts. This involves releasing anger, sadness, and fear, which often requires confronting deep-seated beliefs and emotional patterns. It's about accepting emotions as they are, without judgment or attachment, and allowing them to pass through without letting them define our actions or sense of self.

## Letting Go of the Ego

At a deeper level, letting go involves the release of ego — the sense of a separate, individual self. In many spiritual traditions, the ego is the primary barrier to spiritual growth. Letting go of the ego doesn't mean losing one's identity but recognizing the interconnectedness of all beings and the illusion of separation.

## Practical Aspects of Letting Go

Practising letting go is an individual journey and can manifest in various forms. It often involves a combination of mindfulness, meditation, and other spiritual practices. Mindfulness teaches us to observe our thoughts and feelings without attachment, while meditation provides space and clarity for more profound release.

## Challenges and Misconceptions

One of the significant challenges in practising letting go is confronting deeply ingrained habits and cultural conditioning. The fear of loss, the need for control, and the desire for certainty are potent forces that can hinder this process. Additionally, there are misconceptions about letting go of a passive or indifferent state. In reality, it is an active process of awareness and conscious choice.

## Impact on Relationships and Society

Letting go can profoundly impact not only individuals but also relationships and society as a whole. By letting go of ego-driven behaviours, individuals can engage in more authentic and compassionate interactions. At a societal level, embracing non-attachment can lead to a more sustainable and equitable world, shifting the focus from consumption and competition to cooperation and shared well-being.

## A Journey Towards Freedom and Peace

Embarking on the path of letting go is a journey towards greater freedom, peace, and spiritual fulfilment. It requires patience, courage, and perseverance. As one progresses on this path, the benefits become increasingly apparent — a sense of liberation, a deeper connection with others, and a more profound understanding of the true nature of reality.

This transformative practice is not a destination but a continuous process of growth and discovery. It invites us to let go of what we think we know, open ourselves to new possibilities, and embrace them.

# *Chapter 2: The Roots of Attachment and Ego*

This chapter delves into the foundational aspects of these two profound concepts that significantly shape human experience. Understanding the roots of attachment and ego is akin to embarking on a journey into the deepest parts of our psyche, uncovering the intricate layers that compose our perceptions, behaviours, and emotional responses.

## The Genesis of Attachment

Our exploration begins by tracing the origins of attachment. Attachment starts forming in the earliest stages of our lives as a psychological and emotional phenomenon. The seeds of attachment are sown in the tender interactions between a child and their caregivers. These initial bonds set the blueprint for connecting with others and the world. But attachment extends beyond our relationships with people and encompasses our ties to possessions, beliefs, and even our past experiences and aspirations. By understanding these early formations, we understand why we cling to certain things, ideas, or individuals and how these attachments influence our journey through life.

## Unraveling the Ego

Turning our attention to the ego, we seek to understand its emergence and development. The ego is often misunderstood and sometimes vilified, yet it plays an essential role in our mental and emotional architecture. It is the centre of our conscious experience, the 'I', that navigates the world's complexities. The ego's development is fascinating, beginning as a mechanism for self-identification and evolving into a complex matrix that governs our interactions and decisions. It is a construct shaped by many factors - from biological underpinnings to societal influences. In this chapter, we will uncover the layers of the ego, examining how it is formed, how it matures, and how it can both empower and hinder us.

## The Interplay Between Attachment and Ego

Perhaps most intriguing is the dynamic interplay between attachment and ego. These two elements, while distinct, are deeply interconnected. The ego often fuels our attachments, urging us to cling to things that bolster our sense of self and security. In return, our attachments reinforce our ego, creating a cycle that can be challenging to break. This symbiotic relationship is complex and multifaceted, influencing everything from our relationships to our life choices and spiritual journey.

## Setting the Stage for Transformation

Understanding the roots of attachment and ego sets the stage for transformation. This chapter is not just an academic exercise but a crucial step in our path to personal growth and spiritual enlightenment. By exploring these foundations, we begin to see the patterns and structures that bind us and equip ourselves with the knowledge to start letting go.

As we journey through this chapter, we invite introspection and reflection. Understanding the roots of attachment and ego is a deeply personal process that resonates uniquely with each individual's experiences and perceptions. It is a journey that promises insight and the potential for profound change.

# Exploring the Origins of Attachment in Early Life Experiences

Attachment, a fundamental aspect of human psychology, is a concept that has captivated psychologists, therapists, and researchers for decades. Its roots are deeply embedded in our earliest experiences, shaping our interactions, relationships, and emotional well-being. This exploration into the origins of attachment in early life experiences aims to unravel the complexities of these initial bonds, offering insight into how they influence our later years.

## The Foundations of Attachment Theory

The foundation of our understanding of attachment comes from the pioneering work of John Bowlby and Mary Ainsworth in the mid-20th century. Bowlby, a British psychologist, was the first to introduce the idea of attachment theory, proposing that the bonds formed between children and their primary caregivers have a lasting impact on their emotional and social development. Through her renowned 'Strange Situation' study, Ainsworth expanded on Bowlby's work, identifying different styles of attachment based on how infants react when separated from and then reunited with their caregiver.

## Early Interactions and Attachment Styles

Attachment styles are typically categorized into secure and insecure types, each stemming from the nature of early interactions with caregivers. A secure attachment develops when a caregiver consistently responds to a child's needs with warmth and sensitivity. This reliability builds a sense of trust and security in the child, forming a solid foundation for healthy emotional and relational development.

In contrast, insecure attachments arise from inconsistent, neglectful, or overly intrusive caregiving. These can be divided into anxious, avoidant, and disorganized attachment styles. Anxious attachment is often the result of inconsistent caregiving, where love and attention are unpredictably given. Avoidant attachment tends to develop when caregivers are emotionally distant or unresponsive. Disorganized attachment, the most distressing, arises in environments of neglect or abuse, where the caregiver is a source of both fear and comfort.

## The Role of Early Attachments in Brain Development

Recent advancements in neuroscience have shed light on the significant impact of early attachment experiences on brain development. The first few years of life are critical for forming neural connections, with long-term implications for emotional regulation, stress response, and social skills. Secure attachments foster an environment that supports healthy brain development, aiding the formation of neural pathways associated with positive emotional experiences and resilience.

Conversely, insecure attachments can lead to altered stress responses and difficulties in emotion regulation. Studies have shown that children with insecure attachments often have heightened cortisol levels, a hormone released in response to stress. These physiological changes can have enduring effects, potentially leading to increased vulnerability to anxiety, depression, and other mental health issues in later life.

## Cultural Influences on Attachment

While the principles of attachment theory are widely accepted, it's crucial to consider cultural variations in caregiving practices and their impact on attachment. Different cultures have diverse norms and values regarding child-rearing, which can influence attachment styles. For instance, in some cultures, a more collective approach to caregiving, where multiple family members are involved, can impact the formation of attachments. Therefore, attachment styles and their outcomes can vary significantly across different cultural contexts, highlighting the need for a more nuanced understanding of attachment from a global perspective.

## Attachment Beyond Early Childhood

While early childhood is a critical period for establishing attachment styles, it's important to note that these styles are not set in stone. Changes in life circumstances, relationships, and therapeutic interventions can influence attachment patterns. For example, a child with an insecure attachment style can develop more secure attachments through stable and supportive relationships later in life. Similarly, therapy and counselling can help individuals understand and work through attachment-related issues, leading to healthier relationships and emotional experiences.

## Attachment and Its Long-Term Impact

The implications of early attachment experiences extend far into adulthood. Securely attached individuals generally find it easier to form stable, trusting relationships and tend to have a more positive self-view. They are often better equipped to handle stress and adversity, displaying resilience in the face of challenges.

On the other hand, individuals with insecure attachment styles may struggle with trust, intimacy, and self-esteem issues. They might find it challenging to form close relationships or may exhibit clingy or emotionally distant behaviours in relationships. Understanding one's attachment style can be crucial in personal growth and in seeking therapeutic support to address and work through these challenges.

## Attachment in the Broader Context of Development

It's essential to recognize that attachment is just one piece of the complex puzzle of human development. Genetics, temperament, and environmental influences like socioeconomic status and education also play significant roles. Therefore, while attachment offers valuable insights into emotional and relational development, it should be considered within the broader context of these multifaceted influences.

## Attachment, A Lifelong Influence

The study of attachment in early life experiences provides profound insights into human behaviour and relationships. It underscores the importance of the earlier years in shaping our emotional landscape and highlights the potential for growth and change throughout life. By understanding the roots of our attachment styles, we can gain deeper self-awareness, leading to more fulfilling and healthy relationships. This awareness also empowers us to break cycles of negative relational patterns, paving the way for emotional healing and growth.

The exploration of attachment is an academic endeavour and a journey into the heart of human experience. It sheds light on the intricate dance of emotions, behaviours, and relationships that define our lives, offering a path to understanding and transformation.

# Shaping Identity and Perception in Human Development

The concept of the ego, a central theme in psychology and spirituality, has been the subject of much analysis and debate. In psychological science, particularly in psychoanalytic theory, and in the broader context of individual identity formation, the ego plays a pivotal role. This article aims to delve into the development of the ego, exploring how it shapes our identity and perceptions and influences our interactions with the world.

## The Ego in Psychoanalytic Theory

The roots of our modern understanding of the ego are found in the psychoanalytic theory of Sigmund Freud. Freud conceptualized the ego as part of a tripartite model of the human psyche, which includes the id (the instinctual, biological drives), the superego (the moral conscience), and the ego itself, which acts as an intermediary between these two often conflicting aspects. The ego is responsible for negotiating the demands of the id and the superego, maintaining a balance that allows for effective functioning in the external world.

## Formation of the Ego in Early Development

The ego development begins in early childhood, as the infant differentiates between the self and the external world. Interactions with caregivers and the environment influence this process. As the child grows, the ego develops defence mechanisms to cope with internal conflicts between instinctual drives, societal expectations, and external realities. These mechanisms, which include repression, denial, projection, and rationalization, play a critical role in shaping an individual's personality and coping strategies.

## Ego and Identity Formation

Identity formation is one of the fundamental roles of the ego. This becomes particularly evident in adolescence as individuals begin to forge their sense of self. Erik Erikson, a developmental psychologist, emphasized the importance of this phase, identifying the crisis of identity vs. role confusion as a critical stage in human development. The ego navigates through various social roles and expectations, integrating them into a coherent sense of identity.

## Perception and Cognitive Functions of the Ego

The ego is deeply involved in perception and cognition. It helps in organizing thoughts and making sense of the world. The perceptual role of the ego is crucial in interpreting and giving meaning to our experiences. It filters our perceptions through the lens of past experiences, current needs, and future aspirations, significantly influencing how we understand and interact with the world around us.

## The Ego in Interpersonal Relationships

The ego plays a critical role in how we relate to others. It mediates our social interactions, balancing our own needs with those of others. The development of empathy, understanding the emotions and perspectives of others, is also part of the ego's function. A well-balanced ego can navigate complex social landscapes effectively, maintaining healthy relationships and adapting to various social contexts.

## Ego Strength and Psychological Resilience

Ego strength, a concept introduced by Heinz Hartmann, refers to the ego's ability to function effectively and maintain emotional stability despite stress and adversity. A strong ego can manage impulses, handle stress, and cope with life's challenges in adaptive ways. Conversely, a weak ego may struggle with these aspects, leading to psychological difficulties.

## Ego and Defense Mechanisms

Defence mechanisms, while often viewed negatively, are crucial ego functions. They protect the individual from psychological distress. However, overreliance on these mechanisms can lead to maladaptive behaviours and hinder emotional growth. Understanding and recognizing one's defence mechanisms is vital to psychological therapy and self-awareness.

## Cultural and Societal Influences on the Ego

The development of the ego is not only a personal journey but is also influenced by cultural and societal factors. Cultural norms and values play a significant role in shaping the ego. For example, individualistic societies emphasize self-reliance and personal achievement, leading to a different ego development than collectivist cultures, where interdependence and community are more valued.

## The Ego in Spirituality

The ego is seen as a barrier to spiritual growth and enlightenment in many spiritual traditions. The focus is often on transcending the ego or minimizing its influence to connect with a higher consciousness or reality. This perspective offers a contrast to the psychological view, highlighting the multifaceted nature of the ego.

### The Ego in Modern Psychology

Contemporary psychology continues to explore the ego, expanding beyond Freudian theory. Cognitive psychology examines how the ego influences thought processes, decision-making, and problem-solving. Social psychology looks at the ego in the context of group dynamics and social perception.

### The Ego's Role in Mental Health

The health of the ego is integral to overall mental health. Issues with ego functioning can manifest in various psychological disorders, such as anxiety, depression, and personality disorders. Therapy often involves strengthening the ego helping individuals develop healthier coping mechanisms and a more robust sense of self.

### The Continuing Evolution of the Ego Concept

As our understanding of the human mind and behaviour evolves, so does our conception of the ego. It remains a central topic in psychology, philosophy, and spirituality, offering unique insights into its nature and functions. In all its complexity, the ego continues to be a subject of fascination, a key to understanding the intricate tapestry of human identity and experience.

# Society and Culture: Architects of Attachment and Ego

In the intricate tapestry of human psychology, societal and cultural influences play a pivotal role in shaping our attachment styles and ego development. These external forces are often subtle, yet their impact is deeply ingrained into our psyche, influencing how we connect with others and perceive ourselves. This article delves into how society and culture reinforce attachment and ego, offering an in-depth analysis of their intertwined dynamics.

### The Cultural Context of Attachment

Attachment, as a psychological concept, is not merely a product of individual experiences but is deeply embedded in the cultural milieu in which a person is raised. Different cultures have distinct approaches to child-rearing and interpersonal relationships, significantly influencing attachment style development.

In Western cultures, for instance, there is a strong emphasis on fostering independence and self-reliance in children. This cultural value can influence the type of attachment formed, often encouraging a more secure attachment style where children feel safe but are also motivated to explore independently. However, this can sometimes veer towards an avoidant attachment style, particularly in environments that overly stress independence and discourage the expression of vulnerability.

Contrastingly, interdependence and familial solid bonds are highly valued in many Eastern or collectivist cultures. Children are often raised in extended family settings and encouraged to develop strong, interconnected relationships. This can foster secure attachment but may also lead to more anxious attachment styles, particularly in cases where there is an excessive emphasis on familial approval and cohesion.

## Societal Reinforcement of Ego

The ego, defined in psychological terms as the conscious sense of self, is significantly shaped by societal influences. How a society structures its values, goals, and definitions of success can profoundly impact the development and expression of the ego.

In individualistic societies, where personal achievement and individual success are highly prized, ego development can lean towards self-enhancement and competition. Such environments can encourage a more pronounced sense of separate identity and may inadvertently promote ego-centric behaviours. The constant pursuit of personal success and recognition can lead to an inflated ego, where self-worth becomes entangled with achievements and external validation.

In contrast, collectivist societies, which emphasize group harmony and community, may encourage a more subdued ego development. The sense of self in such cultures is often closely linked to one's role and status within the community. While this can foster a sense of belonging and reduce overt egoism, it can also suppress individual identity and promote conformist behaviours.

## Media and Consumer Culture's Impact

The media and the broader consumer culture are potent forces in shaping attachment and the ego. With its pervasive reach and influential narratives, the modern media landscape plays a significant role in setting societal norms and expectations. Advertising and consumer culture, in particular, often promote materialism and acquiring goods as pathways to happiness and success, reinforcing material attachments and ego-driven desires.

Social media, a relatively new yet influential aspect of modern culture, has a complex relationship with attachment and ego. It provides platforms for connection and community building, potentially fostering positive attachments. However, it can also feed into insecurities and the comparison trap, exacerbating anxious attachments and ego-driven behaviours as users constantly evaluate their self-worth against the curated images of others' lives.

## Cultural Narratives and Life Scripts

Cultural narratives and life scripts — the stories and expectations that cultures create about the "proper" way to live — also significantly influence attachment and ego development. These narratives can dictate the milestones and pathways deemed acceptable or successful, shaping individuals' goals, aspirations, and relationships. For instance, the pressure to adhere to traditional life scripts, such as marriage and parenthood at certain ages, can influence relationship attachments and how individuals perceive their self-worth and success.

## The Role of Education and Work Environment

Educational systems and work environments, deeply influenced by cultural and societal norms, are also crucial in shaping attachment styles and ego development. Educational practices emphasising competition and individual achievement can foster an ego-centric approach to learning and success. Similarly, work environments prioritising individual performance and competition can reinforce an ego-driven professional identity and promote attachment to career success as a primary measure of self-worth.

## The Impact on Relationships and Interpersonal Dynamics

Societal and cultural influences extend to personal relationships and interpersonal dynamics. Cultural norms around relationships — whether familial, romantic, or social — can significantly influence attachment styles. Societies emphasising autonomy and individual choice may foster more secure but sometimes more superficial relationships, while those that stress community and familial bonds might encourage deeper but more dependent attachments.

## Adapting to Globalization and Cultural Exchange

In an increasingly globalized world, the interaction and blending of different cultural values and societal norms present challenges and opportunities for developing attachment and ego. Exposure to diverse cultural perspectives can lead to a more flexible and adaptive approach to relationships and self-identity. However, it can also lead to conflicts and confusion as traditional norms clash with new ideas and practices.

Understanding the role of society and culture in shaping attachment and ego makes it evident that these psychological constructs are not just products of individual experiences but are deeply influenced by the broader societal and cultural context. Recognizing this interplay is crucial in understanding human behaviour and pursuing psychological and emotional well-being. It invites a wider perspective, considering the individual and the complex social and cultural tapestries in which they are woven.

# *Chapter 3: The Burden of Material Attachments*

This chapter aims to unravel the intricate relationship we share with our possessions and how this connection influences our lives, often in ways we scarcely recognise.

Material attachment refers to the emotional and psychological bond we form with physical objects. This bond can range from a mild preference for specific items to an intense dependency on material possessions for emotional security and personal identity. While material possessions are essential for survival and comfort, overemphasising acquiring and holding onto them can lead to a burdensome relationship with the material world.

To understand the present dynamics of material attachment, it's insightful to glance back at history. Throughout various epochs, material possessions have been seen as a means to survival and symbols of power, status, and identity. In ancient civilizations, the accumulation of wealth and goods was often associated with social With its capitalist economies and consumer culture, the contemporary world status and divine favour. The Industrial Revolution and the advent of consumerism have significantly reshaped our relationship with material possessions, making it a central aspect of civilisation in modern life.

The contemporary world has further intensified material attachment with its capitalist economies and consumer culture. Advertising, marketing, and social media incessantly bombard us with messages that equate happiness and success with acquiring the latest products and trends. This constant exposure creates a cycle of desire and dissatisfaction, where pursuing material goods becomes an endless quest for fulfilment.

From a psychological standpoint, material attachment often fulfils deeper emotional and psychological needs. These can include security, control, self-esteem, and identity. For some, possessions are a tangible measure of success and personal worth. For others, they provide comfort and stability in an unpredictable world.

One of the key areas where material attachment exerts its influence is in forming and expressing identity. In a culture that often values people based on their possessions, what we own becomes a significant part of who we are. This identification with material objects can lead to a superficial understanding of self, where one's value and identity are inextricably linked to external possessions.

While material possessions can bring joy and convenience, an excessive attachment to them can also have emotional costs. It can lead to increased anxiety and stress, particularly with the fear of loss or damage to these possessions. This attachment can also overshadow more fulfilling and meaningful life experiences, redirecting time, energy, and resources towards acquiring and maintaining material goods.

Our relationships with others can also be impacted by material attachment. It can lead to competitive attitudes, envy, and strained relationships, especially in environments where material success is highly valued. Moreover, pursuing material wealth can sometimes come at the expense of nurturing personal relationships and community ties.

On a societal level, widespread material attachment can have significant implications. It can drive unsustainable consumer behaviour for the environment, contributing to overconsumption and ecological degradation. Additionally, it can exacerbate social inequalities, as pursuing material wealth often becomes a marker of social stratification.

In spiritual terms, material attachment is often vemphasisingiewed as a hindrance to personal growth and enlightenment. Many spiritual traditions advocate for a detachment from material possessions, emphasizing the impermanence of the material world and the importance of inner values and experiences.

Understanding and overcoming material attachment is not about renouncing all possessions or living a life of austerity. Instead, it is about finding a healthy balance, where material possessions are appreciated and enjoyed without becoming the centrecentre of one's life and happiness. It involves shifting focus from external acquisitions to internal growth and finding fulfilment in relationships, experiences, and personal development.

As we progress through this chapter, we will explore various dimensions of material attachment, examining its roots, manifestations, and impacts. We will also delve into strategies for developing a healthier relationship with material possessions, paving the way for a more balanced, fulfilling, and sustainable way of living. The journey through understanding material attachment is about changing our relationship with things and transforming our perspectives on what truly matters in life.

# Materialism and Its Impact on the Soul: A Deep Dive into Mental and Spiritual Well-being

Materialism is a pervasive aspect of modern life, defined as a preoccupation or emphasis on material objects and comforts. It shapes how we view the world, relationships, and ourselves. While the pursuit of material wealth and possessions is often seen as a path to happiness and success, the impact of materialism on mental and spiritual well-being is a subject of increasing concern and scrutiny. This article delves into the intricate ways in which materialism affects our inner lives, often in ways we may not immediately recognize.

Pursuing material wealth and possessions is deeply embedded in many cultures and societies. A belief thaPursuingt happiness and contentment often drives it can be attained through acquiring and accumulating. However, this pursuit can lead to a cycle of endless desire and temporary satisfaction, where one acquisition leads to the longing for another. Psychologically, this cycle is known as the hedonic treadmill – a concept suggesting that as people make more money or acquire more things, their expectations and desires rise in tandem, leading to no permanent gain in happiness.

The impact of materialism on mental health is multi-faceted. On the one hand, material wealth can provide security, comfort, and access to life-enhancing opportunities. On the other hand, an excessive focus on material gain can lead to increased stress, anxiety, and feelings of inadequacy. Studies have shown that high levels of materialism are often associated with a range of negative emotions and experiences, including depression, low self-esteem, and a decrease in overall life satisfaction. This is partly because materialism can shift an individual's focus away from intrinsic values, such as personal growth and community connection, towards extrinsic goals, like wealth and status.

Moreover, materialism can impact interpersonal relationships. Relationships may become secondary to the pursuit of material gain, or they may be viewed through the lens of what material benefits they can provide. This transactional view of relationships undermines the deep, meaningful connections essential for psychological well-being. Additionally, materialism can lead to social comparison, where one's self-worth and success are constantly measured against others. This comparison can create feelings of jealousy, inadequacy, and discontent.

From a spiritual perspective, materialism presents a different set of challenges. Many spiritual traditions emphasise the impermanence of the material world and advocate for a detachment from physical possessions. They argue that true contentment and fulfilment come from inner spiritual growth, community, and connection to something greater than oneself. In this view, materialism can be seen as a distraction or a barrier to spiritual development. It can create an external focus, where one's time and energy are directed towards acquiring and maintaining possessions rather than inward reflection and spiritual practices.

Pursuing material wealth can also lead to ethical and moral dilemmas that conflict with spiritual values. For instance, the desire for more can sometimes lead to behaviours that clash with the principles of fairness, honesty, and compassion. This conflict can create internal dissonance and spiritual unrest.

One of the more subtle ways materialism affects spiritual well-being is through its impact on gratitude and appreciation. When the focus is always on acquiring more, it can be challenging to appreciate and be grateful for what one already has. Gratitude is crucial to spiritual well-being, fostering a sense of contentment, peace, and connection with the world. By its very nature, materialism can erode this sense of gratitude, replacing it with a feeling of perpetual wanting.

However, it's essential to recognize that material possessions, in themselves, are not inherently harmful. They can provide comfort, security, and enjoyment. The key lies in our relationship with these possessions. They can lead to the issues described above when seen as the primary source of happiness and self-worth. Conversely, when viewed as tools to support one's life goals and values rather than as goals in themselves, their impact on mental and spiritual well-being can be more balanced and positive.

In conclusion, the relationship between materialism and mental and spiritual well-being is complex and multifaceted. While material possessions can bring comfort and pleasure, an excessive focus on them can lead to adverse mental health outcomes and hinder spiritual growth. Understanding and moderating our relationship with material possessions can be crucial to achieving a more balanced, fulfilling life. Trecognisinghis involves recognizing the transient nature of material goods, focusing on intrinsic values, and cultivating gratitude, enhancing our mental and spiritual well-being.

## Wealth and Want: How Socioeconomic Backgrounds Shape Our Material World

The complex relationship between socioeconomic factors and material attachment is significant in understanding human behaviour and well-being. Critical economic status, which encompasses income, educational attainment, occupational prestige, and social status, significantly influences attitudes towards material possessions. This article aims to delve into how varying socioeconomic backgrounds shape our relationships with material goods and how these relationships, in turn, affect our mental and spiritual health.

At the heart of this discussion is the concept that material attachment isn't solely a matter of personal choice or preference but is deeply entwined with the broader socioeconomic context in which individuals live. This context determines access to resources, exposure to certain lifestyles, and internalising specific values and aspirations.

## Influence of Socioeconomic Status on Material Values

Individuals from higher socioeconomic backgrounds often have greater access to material resources. This abundance can lead to different attitudes towards possessions than those from lower economic backgrounds. In affluent settings, there can be a tendency to see material possessions as markers of success and status. The availability and abundance of resources can sometimes lead to a sense of entitlement and a consumerist attitude, where acquiring new and better possessions becomes a normative behaviour. However, this relationship is not linear or straightforward. Individuals raised in wealth might sometimes develop a sense of responsibility towards their resources, focusing on sustainability and ethical consumption.

Conversely, those from lower socioeconomic backgrounds may view material possessions differently due to their limited access to resources. For some, material goods might represent security and stability – something not always guaranteed. As a result, there can be a stronger emotional attachment to possessions, with each item holding significant value and meaning. Alternatively, a lack of resources can foster a sense of resilience and an ability to find contentment and joy in non-material aspects of life, such as community, relationships, and creativity.

The impact of material attachment on mental health can vary considerably across different socioeconomic spectra. In affluent societies or groups, the pressure to maintain or enhance one's status through material possessions can lead to stress, anxiety, and feelings of inadequacy. The constant comparison with others and the pursuit of an idealized lifestyle can erode mental well-being and direct to a range of psychological issues, including depression and chronic dissatisfaction.

For individuals from lower socioeconomic backgrounds, the challenges are often different. The stress related to securing necessities can be a significant source of anxiety and worry. When material possessions are linked to survival and essential comfort, their loss or absence can have a profound impact on mental health. Additionally, the stigma and social exclusion associated with poverty can exacerbate feelings of low self-esteem and hopelessness.

## Socioeconomic Status and Spiritual Well-being

The influence of socioeconomic factors extends to spiritual well-being as well. In affluent contexts, where materialism is prevalent, there can be a spiritual void as material pursuits overshadow deeper spiritual needs and values. The relentless pursuit of material wealth can lead to a disconnection from one's inner self and the broader community, resulting in spiritual emptiness.

In contrast, individuals from lower SES backgrounds often develop a rich sense of community and interconnectedness, which can be spiritually fulfilling. The scarcity challenges can also lead to a deeper appreciation for non-material aspects of life, fostering a sense of gratitude, resilience, and a solid connection to one's values and beliefs.

## Cultural and Societal Implications

The relationship between socioeconomic status and material attachment also has broader cultural and societal implications. Societies emphasising material success and consumerism often witness higher levels of social inequality and environmental degradation. Conversely, cultures that value simplicity and non-materialistic lifestyles promote more sustainable and equitable ways of living.

## Balancing Material and Non-Material Aspects of Life

Navigating the complex relationship between socioeconomic factors and material attachment requires a balanced approach. It involves recognizing the role of material possessions in providing comfort and security while also understanding their limitations in bringing lasting happiness and fulfilment. This balance is crucial for both mental and spiritual well-being.

Fostering this balance may involve various strategies, such as cultivating gratitude, focusing on experiences rather than possessions, and developing a sense of purpose and connection that transcends material achievements. It also involves a societal shift towards valuing personal qualities, relationships, and community over material wealth.

The interplay between socioeconomic factors and material attachment is a multifaceted issue with significant mental and spiritual well-being implications. Understanding this relationship is crucial in addressing the challenges of materialism and fostering a more balanced, fulfilling life. It requires a collective effort to redefine success and happiness holistically, moving beyond material possessions to embrace the richness of human experience in all its forms.

# The Role of Education and Awareness in Redefining Material Values

Education is pivotal in shaping our understanding and attitudes towards material possessions. Educational systems that emphasize critical thinking, ethical considerations, and holistic well-being can help inculcate values that transcend materialism. By integrating discussions about consumerism's psychological, social, and environmental impacts into curricula, we can nurture a more conscious and responsible approach towards material consumption from a young age.

Awareness campaigns and community programs are crucial in redefining material values. These initiatives can focus on the benefits of minimalism, the joy of giving, and the importance of sustainability. They can help shift the focus from what we own to who we are and how we contribute to our communities and the world.

### The Psychological Shift: From Scarcity to Abundance Mindset

Another critical aspect is the psychological shift from a scarcity mindset, which focuses on what we lack, to an abundance mindset, which appreciates what we have. This shift is crucial in both high and low economic groups. For those in higher Economic groups, it can mean recognising that fulfilment doesn't solely come from acquiring more but from appreciating and utilizing what one already possesses. For lower Economic groups, it involves finding richness in non-material aspects of life, such as relationships, community, and personal growth.

In today's digital era, where online shopping and digital marketing are at our fingertips, understanding and managing material attachment becomes even more complex. The ease of acquiring goods and the bombardment of targeted advertising can intensify material desires. Developing digital literacy and self-regulation in the use of technology is crucial in mitigating the impact of these influences on our material values.

From a spiritual perspective, reconnecting with our inner values and understanding the transient nature of material possessions can offer a path to liberation from material attachment. Spiritual practices like meditation, mindfulness, and community service can provide a sense of fulfilment and purpose that material possessions cannot.

This spiritual approach doesn't necessitate renouncing material possessions but cultivating a healthy relationship with them. It involves recognizing possessions as tools to facilitate life's journey rather than the destination itself. This mindset can lead to a more balanced and contented life, where material possessions serve our needs without dominating our values and self-worth.

Socioeconomic mobility, or the ability to move between different social and economic strata, also influences material attachment. The experience of shifting from a lower to a higher socioeconomic status, or vice versa, can profoundly impact one's views on material possessions. Those who experience upward mobility may develop a different appreciation for material goods, seeing them as symbols of their hard work and achievement. Conversely, downward mobility can lead to reevaluating what truly matters in life, often shifting focus from material wealth to relationships and personal resilience.

Lastly, policy and economic systems can influence material attachment by shaping the financial landscape people navigate. Policies that address income inequality provide access to education and health care, and promote sustainable development can help create an environment where material attachment is not driven by necessity or status but is a matter of informed personal choice.

Economic systems that prioritize people and the planet over profit and encourage sustainable and ethical consumption can also significantly shape attitudes towards material possessions. By creating systems that value well-being and sustainability, we can foster a culture that balances material attachment with social responsibility and environmental stewardship.

The relationship between socioeconomic factors and material attachment is intricate and multi-dimensional. Various factors influence it, including cultural norms, psychological motivations, educational systems, and economic structures. Understanding this relationship is essential in addressing the challenges of materialism and promoting a more balanced and fulfilling approach to life. By redefining our relationship with material possessions and focusing on what truly enriches our lives, we can foster greater well-being, individually and collectively. This shift requires a concerted effort across multiple domains, from individual awareness and education to policy and societal change, underscoring the need for a holistic approach to addressing the complexities of material attachment.

# Youth in the Age of Materialism

Understanding how material attachment affects younger generations is crucial in an era marked by rapid technological advancement and consumer culture. The influences of upbringing, media, and peer pressure play pivotal roles in shaping the attitudes and behaviours of children and adolescents towards material possessions. This exploration seeks to unravel the complex web of factors contributing to material attachment in younger generations and how it impacts their development and well-being.

### Upbringing and Family Influence

The foundation of a child's attitude towards material possessions often begins in the home. Family upbringing plays a significant role in shaping a child's values and perceptions regarding material wealth. Parents and caregivers are the primary role models for children, and their attitudes towards possessions, money, and consumption inevitably influence the child's perspective. Children are likely to develop similar beliefs in families where material possessions are highly valued and equated with success or happiness.

Moreover, how parents use material goods can impact a child's development of material attachment. For instance, using material possessions as rewards or substitutes for emotional nurturing can lead to an association between material goods and emotional fulfilment. Conversely, families that emphasize non-material values, such as experiences, relationships, and personal achievement, may foster a more balanced view in their children regarding the role of material possessions in life.

## Media Influences and Consumer Culture

The media is a powerful influence on younger generations, shaping their perceptions and desires. Advertisements, television shows, movies, and, more recently, social media are replete with images and messages that glorify materialism. They often portray a lifestyle where happiness, success, and popularity are closely tied to owning certain products or brands.

Social media, in particular, has amplified this effect. Platforms like Instagram, TikTok, and Snapchat are flooded with influencers and celebrities showcasing luxurious lifestyles, the latest gadgets, fashion, and more. For young people, constantly exposed to these images, the line between reality and the curated personas on social media can blur, leading to unrealistic expectations and a heightened desire for material possessions.

## Peer Pressure and Social Dynamics

Peer influence is another significant factor in developing material attachment among youth. During adolescence, the opinion of peers becomes increasingly important, often surpassing family influence. Material possessions can become symbols of social status and acceptance in this social landscape. Owning the latest smartphone, wearing specific brands, or possessing other trendy items can be considered a social inclusion and popularity prerequisite.

The need to belong and be accepted can drive young people to prioritise material possessions more than their intrinsic values. This dynamic can create pressure to conform to worldly norms, leading to increased anxiety and stress, especially among those who cannot afford these possessions.

## The Psychological Impact of Material Attachment

The effects of material attachment on young people's mental health are multifaceted. While material possessions can bring temporary joy and satisfaction, overemphasising them can lead to various psychological issues. These include decreased self-esteem, heightened anxiety, and a persistent sense of inadequacy.

Moreover, when self-worth is tied to material possessions, it can lead to a fragile sense of self dependent on external validation. This dependence can hinder the development of intrinsic motivation and resilience, critical factors for long-term well-being and success.

## Materialism and Values Development

Material attachment also impacts the development of values in younger generations. In a culture emphasising material success, values such as compassion, community, and altruism may take a backseat. This shift can affect how young people interact with their peers, form relationships, and make decisions. It can lead to a more self-centred worldview, prioritising personal gain over collective well-being.

## Navigating the Material World: Strategies for Balance

Addressing the challenges of material attachment in younger generations requires a multi-faceted approach. It involves parents and educators fostering environments where intrinsic values are celebrated and material possessions are viewed in a balanced perspective.

Educational programs promoting media literacy can equip young people with the skills to analyze the messages they receive from various media sources critically. Discussions around consumerism, sustainability, and ethical consumption can also help develop a more conscious and responsible approach to material possessions.

Furthermore, creating spaces for young people to engage in meaningful activities and relationships that are not centered around material possessions can provide alternatives to worldly pursuits. These activities can include community service, arts, sports, and other pursuits that foster a sense of accomplishment and fulfilment beyond material acquisition.

The impact of material attachment on younger generations is a complex issue intertwined with family dynamics, media influence, and peer pressure. Navigating this landscape requires awareness, education, and support from families, educators, and the community. By fostering environments that value personal growth, relationships, and intrinsic achievements over material possessions, we can help young people develop healthier relationships with the material world and build a foundation for long-term well-being.

# Embracing Simplicity and Non-Attachment: Lessons from Spiritual Traditions"

In a world increasingly dominated by materialism and consumer culture, the ancient teachings of various spiritual traditions on simplicity and non-attachment stand as beacons of wisdom. Though rooted in diverse cultures and philosophies, these teachings converge on the fundamental idea that true peace and happiness lie not in the accumulation of material possessions but in embracing a more straightforward, more detached way of life. This article delves into the profound insights different spiritual traditions offer on simplicity and non-attachment, exploring how these concepts can enrich our lives in the modern world.

## Buddhism: The Path of Non-Attachment

With its profound teachings on the nature of suffering and liberation, Buddhism places significant emphasis on non-attachment. According to Buddhist philosophy, attachment to material possessions, desires, thoughts, and emotions is a primary source of human suffering. This is encapsulated in the concept of Dukkha, which represents the inherent unsatisfactoriness of life when desires and attachments bind one.

The Buddhist path advocates for a middle way that balances severe asceticism and indulgence in worldly pleasures. Central to this path is mindfulness, which involves being fully present and aware of one's thoughts, feelings, and actions without clinging or aversion. By cultivating non-attachment, individuals can free themselves from the cycle of desire and suffering, achieving inner peace and enlightenment.

## Hinduism: Detachment and the Pursuit of Truth

In Hinduism, the concept of non-attachment, or Vairagya, is pivotal in pursuing spiritual knowledge and liberation (Moksha). The teachings emphasize that attachment to the material world, including one's body, possessions, and social status, can entangle the soul in the cycle of rebirth and suffering.

The Bhagavad Gita, a sacred Hindu scripture, speaks eloquently about the practice of detachment. Lord Krishna advises Arjuna to perform his duties with dedication but without attachment to the results, a concept known as Karma Yoga. This detachment is not a disengagement from the world but a deeper understanding of the transient nature of material reality and a focus on the eternal spiritual truth.

## Christianity: Simplicity and the Virtue of Poverty

Christian teachings, particularly in the Gospels, often highlight the virtue of simplicity and the dangers of material wealth. Jesus Christ's life and teachings serve as a model for living simply and humbly. The Beatitudes, for example, bless the poor in spirit, emphasizing the spiritual richness found in simplicity and humility.

Many Christian saints and mystics have extolled the virtues of a simple life, free from excessive material possessions. St. Francis of Assisi, known for his deep love of nature and commitment to poverty, saw simplicity as a way to come closer to God and appreciate creation's beauty in its purest form.

## Islam: Moderation and Trust in God

Islamic teachings advocate for a life of moderation and balance, avoiding both extravagance and miserliness. The Quran encourages Muslims to use their wealth wisely and responsibly, seeing it as a trust from God. The idea of Zakat, one of the Five Pillars of Islam, involves giving a portion of one's wealth to people in need, fostering a sense of detachment from material possessions and a spirit of generosity.

Sufism, the mystical branch of Islam, delves deeper into the concept of detachment. Sufi teachings emphasize Tawakkul, or trust in God, which includes relinquishing one's ego and worldly desires to fully depend on and connect with the Divine.

## Taoism: Harmony with Nature and Simplicity

Taoism, an ancient Chinese philosophy and spiritual path, teaches the principle of living in harmony with the Tao (the Way or the natural order of the universe). This involves embracing simplicity and spontaneity, aligning one's life with the natural flow of the world.

The Taoist concept of Wu Wei, or non-action, is not about inactivity but finding the simplest, most effortless way of living that is in harmony with nature. This includes letting go of unnecessary desires and ambitions, and finding contentment in the simplicity and beauty of the natural world.

## Modern Implications of Simplicity and Non-Attachment

In today's fast-paced, consumer-driven world, the teachings of simplicity and non-attachment from various spiritual traditions offer a counter-narrative. They invite us to reevaluate our relationship with material possessions and consider the impact of our lifestyle choices on our mental, spiritual, and environmental well-being.

Embracing simplicity and non-attachment does not necessarily mean rejecting all material possessions or leading an ascetic life. Instead, it involves cultivating a sense of contentment and peace, recognizing that true happiness and fulfilment come from within, not external sources. This perspective encourages us to live more mindfully and sustainably, valuing experiences, relationships, and inner growth over material accumulation.

The teachings on simplicity and non-attachment from various spiritual traditions offer timeless wisdom that is increasingly relevant in our contemporary context. They challenge us to reflect on our priorities and values, guiding us towards a more fulfilling and meaningful way of life. By incorporating these principles into our daily lives, we can find more excellent balance, peace, and harmony within ourselves and the world around us.

# Beyond Possessions: Embracing Lifestyles of Minimalism, Simplicity, and Sharing

In a world where consumerism and material accumulation often dominate, alternative lifestyles and philosophies that challenge the materialistic norm are gaining traction. These approaches, including minimalism, voluntary simplicity, and the sharing economy, offer pathways to a more meaningful, less cluttered, and socially conscious way of living. This article explores these alternatives to materialism, delving into their principles, practices, and the benefits they bring to individual lives and society.

## Minimalism: The Art of Less

Minimalism as a lifestyle choice is centred around living with less. This doesn't merely mean having fewer possessions but also encompasses a broader philosophy of reducing life's clutter to focus on what's truly important. Minimalists advocate for a lifestyle that values quality over quantity, concentrating on experiences and relationships rather than material possessions.

The minimalist movement challenges the conventional consumerist narrative that more is better. Instead, it posits that reducing physical clutter can lead to a clearer mind, decreased stress, and a more focused life. By consciously choosing to own fewer possessions, minimalists find that they can dedicate more time, energy, and resources to the things that genuinely bring joy and fulfilment.

One of the most compelling aspects of minimalism is its versatility. It doesn't prescribe a one-size-fits-all approach but allows individuals to define what minimalism means for them. For some, it might mean living in a small, sparsely furnished space with only the essentials. For others, it could involve decluttering and streamlining their belongings to create a more organized and peaceful living environment.

## Voluntary Simplicity: Choosing a Richer Life

Voluntary simplicity is a lifestyle choice that emphasizes living more meaningfully with less. It's about choosing a less complicated life, focusing on non-material aspects of well-being like relationships, community, personal growth, and environmental responsibility. Voluntary simplicity isn't about living in deprivation but finding richness in experiences that don't revolve around material accumulation.

This lifestyle encourages individuals to question mainstream consumer culture and make conscious choices about living and consuming. It involves reassessing priorities, values, and the impact of one's lifestyle choices on the world. People embracing this philosophy often find greater satisfaction in simpler pleasures, like nature, art, and human connection, than material goods.

One key component of voluntary simplicity is mindfulness in consumption. This means being aware of the environmental and social impact of one's purchasing choices and opting for sustainable, ethical products. It also involves reducing waste and resourcefulness, principles that align closely with environmental conservation efforts.

## The Sharing Economy: Community and Collaboration

The sharing economy represents a shift from the traditional individual ownership model towards a shared access and collaborative consumption system. This economic model leverages technology to facilitate sharing resources, such as cars, homes, tools, and skills, among individuals.

Platforms like car-sharing services, home rental sites, and tool libraries exemplify the sharing economy. These platforms promote a more efficient and sustainable use of goods by providing access to resources without the need for ownership. The sharing economy reduces the demand for producing new goods, thereby lessening environmental impact and fostering community and connectedness among participants.

An essential aspect of the sharing economy is its potential to democratize resource access. By making goods and services more accessible and affordable, it can play a role in reducing economic inequality. Additionally, it encourages a culture of trust and cooperation, challenging the traditional norms of competition and individualism.

## Benefits of Alternative Lifestyles

Adopting lifestyles like minimalism, voluntary simplicity, and sharing economy participation can have profound benefits. On a personal level, these lifestyles can lead to reduced stress, greater financial freedom, and more time and energy for personal passions and relationships. They often result in a greater sense of purpose and fulfilment as individuals find meaning beyond material possessions.

From an environmental perspective, these lifestyle choices can significantly reduce one's ecological footprint. By consuming less, sharing more, and making sustainable choices, individuals contribute to a healthier planet. This shift in consumption patterns can also drive broader changes in the market, encouraging businesses to adopt more sustainable practices.

## Challenges and Considerations

While these alternative lifestyles offer numerous benefits, they also come with challenges. Breaking free from deeply ingrained consumerist habits and societal expectations can be difficult. There can be social pressures to conform to traditional norms of success and material wealth, making these alternative paths seem counter-cultural.

Furthermore, it's essential to recognize that the ability to choose these lifestyles can be a privilege unavailable to everyone. For some, living with less is not a choice but a necessity due to economic constraints. Thus, promoting these lifestyles requires sensitivity to different socioeconomic realities.

In a world where materialism often overshadows other values, lifestyles like minimalism, voluntary simplicity, and the sharing economy offer refreshing alternatives. They encourage us to rethink our relationship with material possessions, focus on what truly matters, and live more sustainably and more fulfilling. By embracing these philosophies, individuals can contribute to a cultural shift towards more mindful, responsible, and community-oriented ways of living.

# *Chapter 4: The Illusions of the Ego*

In the quest to understand the self, one of the most intriguing and, at times, perplexing concepts we encounter is the ego. This chapter invites you to explore this elusive concept, not merely as a psychological construct but as a pivotal element in the tapestry of human experience. This exploration transcends the boundaries of psychology, venturing into the rich realms of spiritual traditions and philosophical thought, where the ego is often seen not just as a component of the mind, but as a fundamental barrier to true understanding and fulfilment.

In its simplest form, the ego can be thought of as the sense of self or 'I' that each person experiences. Our subjective consciousness is the part of us that perceives, interacts with, and attempts to make sense of the world. In the modern psychological context, the ego is recognized as an essential part of the human psyche, mediating between our primitive desires and the demands of the external world. It helps us navigate through life, make decisions, and form our identity. However, this understanding of the ego is just the tip of the iceberg.

The ego takes on a different shade of meaning in various spiritual traditions. The ego takes on a distinct shade of meaning in diverse spiritual traditions. It is often portrayed as a source of illusion, a barrier that separates us from a deeper understanding of reality. For instance, in Buddhism, the concept of Anatta, or 'no-self', challenges the existence of a permanent, unchanging ego. According to this view, the belief in a fixed self is a source of suffering, and true liberation comes from realizing the impermanent and interconnected nature of all things.

Similarly, Hindu philosophy speaks of the ego as Ahamkara, an aspect of the mind that creates a sense of individuality and separateness. This separation is seen as an illusion, a veil obscuring our true nature, Atman, or the universal self. The Bhagavad Gita, a seminal Hindu text, expounds on the need to transcend the ego to attain spiritual enlightenment and union with the divine.

In Taoism, the ego is viewed as a construct that disrupts the natural flow of life. The Tao Te Ching, the foundational text of Taoism, advocates for a state of egolessness, where one aligns with the Tao, or the way of the universe, achieving harmony and balance. This alignment requires letting go of the ego's rigid control and embracing the spontaneity and simplicity of life.

Yet, despite these spiritual admonitions, the ego is a persistent and pervasive aspect of our existence. It manifests in countless ways in everyday life, influencing how we perceive ourselves and others, shaping our relationships, and guiding our actions. The ego can drive our ambitions and achievements but can also lead to conflict, suffering, and a distorted perception of reality.

One of the most significant ways the ego manifests is through the desire for recognition and validation. This desire can become a driving force in our lives, dictating our choices and actions. It often leads to a comparison with others, creating feelings of superiority or inferiority, jealousy, and discontent. The ego can make us cling to rigid beliefs and identities, causing resistance to change and growth.

The influence of the ego extends to our relationships as well. It can lead to conflicts, as the need to be right or to assert one's viewpoint overshadows the need for understanding and connection. In contrast, when the ego is balanced, it allows for more harmonious relationships, where empathy and compassion precede the need for control and validation.

Recognizing and observing the ego can be a challenging yet transformative process. It requires self-awareness and mindfulness, allowing us to see the ego in action without immediately reacting. This awareness is the first step in loosening the ego's grip on our perception and behaviour. This chapter will introduce various exercises and meditations designed to help you observe and understand your ego. These practices are not about eradicating the ego, which is impossible, but about finding a balance where the ego serves us without dominating our lives.

In this chapter, we will also delve into how the understanding of the ego can be applied to modern challenges. In an age dominated by social media and the pursuit of external validation, understanding the role of the ego is more critical than ever. We will explore how the ego interacts with technology, social norms, and the pressures of contemporary life.

This chapter is more than an exploration of a psychological or spiritual concept; it is a journey into self-understanding. By examining the various facets of the ego, from its psychological functions to its spiritual implications, we aim to provide a comprehensive understanding of this complex aspect of the human experience. This understanding can lead to a more balanced, fulfilling, and enlightened way of living, where the ego is recognized not as a master but as a part of the more extraordinary tapestry of our lives.

## Tracing the Ego Through Time: A Historical Perspective on a Pivotal Concept

The ego concept, central to psychology and philosophy, has undergone significant evolution throughout history. This journey, spanning various cultures and philosophical landscapes, reveals how our understanding of the self or ego has shifted and expanded. This article aims to trace the historical trajectory of the ego, examining key moments and thinkers that have shaped our current understanding of this essential aspect of human identity.

The story of the ego begins in the ancient world, where philosophical inquiries into the nature of self and identity first emerged. In ancient Eastern philosophies, the concept of the self was often explored in relation to the universe and existence. Hindu scriptures like the Upanishads, written around 800 BCE, ponder the nature of Atman (self) and its relationship to Brahman, the universal soul. The self is not an isolated entity but part of a larger, interconnected reality.

In ancient Greece, similar inquiries were taking place. Through his dialectical method, Socrates sought to understand the essence of human qualities, pushing the boundaries of self-knowledge. His famous dictum, "Know thyself," reflects the importance placed on understanding one's inner nature. Following him, Plato's ideas about the tripartite soul divided the self into logical, spirited, and appetitive parts, a precursor to later concepts of the ego.

The evolution of the ego concept continued through the works of St. Augustine in the 4th century AD, who introduced introspection as a way to understand the self. His Confessions represent one of the first detailed explorations of the inner workings of the mind and the self, laying the groundwork for later psychological analysis.

However, in the Enlightenment period, the concept of the ego began to take a more defined shape. René Descartes' famous declaration, "Cogito, ergo sum" (I think, therefore I am), in the 17th century, placed the thinking self at the the center of philosophy. Descartes' idea of a thinking ego as the foundation of identity and existence marked a significant shift towards a more individualistic view of the self.

The 18th and 19th centuries saw a further expansion of the concept. Immanuel Kant's works delved into the nature of the self, distinguishing between the empirical self, experienced through our senses, and the 'noumenal' self, which is inaccessible to sensory perception. His ideas influenced the development of German idealism, which further explored the nature of self-consciousness.

The 19th century marked the emergence of psychology as a distinct scientific discipline, with the ego becoming a central topic of study. Sigmund Freud's psychoanalytic theory was groundbreaking in the late 19th and early 20th centuries. Freud conceptualized the ego as part of a complex mind structure, including the id (instinctual desires) and the superego (moral conscience). For Freud, the ego was the seat of consciousness and played a crucial role in mediating between the demands of the id, the superego, and reality.

Carl Jung, a contemporary of Freud, expanded the understanding of the ego in his analytical psychology. Jung saw the ego as the centre of consciousness but differentiated it from the self, encompassing both conscious and unconscious elements. Jung's exploration of archetypes and the collective unconscious further enriched the concept of the ego.

In the 20th century, existentialist philosophers like Jean-Paul Sartre and Martin Heidegger delved into the nature of existence and identity, focusing on individual experience and the self's relation to the world. Sartre, in particular, explored the idea of the ego as a construct, a creation of consciousness and not its precondition.

Meanwhile, Eastern philosophies continued to offer alternative perspectives. The mid-20th century saw a surge in interest in Eastern spiritual traditions, which often view the ego as an illusion or barrier to spiritual enlightenment. This perspective influenced Western psychotherapy, leading to integrative approaches that combine Eastern and Western understandings of the self.

Today, the concept of the ego is as relevant as ever, continuing to evolve with new insights from psychology, neuroscience, and philosophy. It remains a central theme in identity, consciousness, and human behaviour discussions.

In conclusion, the historical evolution of the concept of the ego is a testament to humanity's ongoing quest to understand itself. From ancient philosophical inquiries to modern psychological theories, the ego's journey reflects our ever-changing views on what it means to be human. This rich tapestry of ideas and theories helps us comprehend the ego's complexity and offers valuable insights into the broader human experience.

# The Many Faces of Ego: A Cultural Tapestry of Self-Understanding

Throughout human history, the concept of the ego has been a subject of profound interest and varied interpretation across different cultures. This intricate mosaic of understandings and approaches offers a unique window into how diverse societies perceive the self. This article seeks to conduct a comparative analysis of the ego across cultures, exploring the universalities and distinctions that mark our understanding of this complex facet of human identity.

In Western thought, particularly within the psychology framework, the ego is often conceptualized as the center of consciousness, responsible for thoughts, decisions, and interactions with the external world. Rooted in the works of Freud and Jung, the Western interpretation of the ego is closely tied to individual identity, personal autonomy, and rationality. This perspective sees the ego as a key player in personal development, often emphasizing the importance of strengthening and understanding the ego for achieving psychological well-being.

Contrastingly, many Eastern philosophies and spiritual traditions present a different viewpoint. In these cultures, the ego is frequently viewed as an obstacle to true understanding and enlightenment. For instance, in Buddhism, the concept of Anatta, or 'no-self', asserts that the idea of a permanent, unchanging self is an illusion. This perspective does not negate the existence of a personal experience but suggests that clinging to the ego-self leads to suffering. The Buddhist path, therefore, involves practices aimed at dissolving the ego's grip, enabling a realization of interconnectedness with all beings.

Similarly, Hindu teachings discuss the concept of Ahamkara, the ego-mind, which is seen as the source of self-identification and attachment to personal history and physical existence. In Hindu philosophy, transcending Ahamkara is essential for realizing the Atman, or true self, which is eternal and beyond individual identity. This view encourages a detachment from the ego and a pursuit of a higher, more universal identity.

The perspective on the ego in Taoism, the ancient Chinese philosophy, also contrasts with Western views. Taoism advocates for a state of egolessness, where one aligns with the Tao, the universe's natural order. This alignment involves letting go of forced efforts and desires driven by the ego, and embracing a life of simplicity and spontaneity instead. The ego is seen as a source of imbalance and disharmony with the natural world.

Understanding the self and ego in Indigenous cultures often emphasizes a deep connection with the community and the environment. Many Indigenous philosophies view the self as inherently linked to one's community, ancestors, and the natural world, rather than as an isolated entity. In this context, the ego is not the center of consciousness but a part of a larger, interdependent system. This perspective fosters a sense of responsibility towards others and the environment, with the ego taking a more communal and integrative role.

The African concept of Ubuntu, which translates to "I am because we are," reflects a similar communal understanding of identity. In this worldview, the self is understood through relationships with others, and the ego is not seen as an isolated, independent entity. The emphasis is on harmony, cooperation, and the community's well-being, which contrasts with more individualistic interpretations of the ego in Western thought.

In modern times, globalization and cross-cultural exchanges have led to a blending of these diverse perspectives on the ego. The Western emphasis on individualism and personal identity is being increasingly balanced with Eastern and Indigenous views that highlight interconnectedness and the transcendence of the ego.

This comparative analysis reveals that while the concept of the ego has universal elements, its interpretation and significance vary greatly across cultures. In some, the ego is a central aspect of personal development and identity, while in others, it is seen as an illusion or barrier to deeper understanding and communal harmony. These diverse perspectives offer valuable insights into the human experience, reminding us that understanding and relating to the ego can profoundly shape our approach to life, relationships, and personal growth.

Understanding the ego through this cultural lens enriches our comprehension of self and fosters a greater appreciation for the diversity of human thought. It challenges us to look beyond our cultural paradigms and consider alternative ways of perceiving the self. In doing so, we open ourselves to a more holistic and integrated understanding of what it means to be human, which embraces the many faces of the ego in its myriad cultural expressions.

## Unveiling the Ego in Spiritual Traditions

While familiar in the realm of psychology, the concept of the ego takes on profound and diverse dimensions within various spiritual traditions. These traditions, each with its unique worldview, offer deep insights into the nature of the ego, its role in human experience, and the path to transcendence. This article explores the intricate perspectives on the ego in several key spiritual traditions, providing a comprehensive understanding of this complex and pivotal concept.

## The Ego in Buddhism: The Illusion of Self

In Buddhism, the ego is often discussed in the context of Anatta, or 'no-self'. This fundamental doctrine posits that the idea of a permanent, unchanging self is an illusion. Unlike many Western philosophies that consider the self or ego as a central, enduring entity, Buddhism teaches that what we perceive as the 'self' is merely a collection of changing phenomena, including feelings, perceptions, and mental formations.

This perspective implies that clinging to the ego – the idea of a solid, independent self – is a source of suffering. The Buddhist path involves recognizing the transient nature of the ego and its desires. Through meditation and mindfulness, one learns to observe the arising and passing of thoughts and feelings without attachment, leading to a state of liberation, free from the ego's delusions.

## Hinduism: Ego and the Path to Enlightenment

In Hinduism, the concept of ego, or Ahamkara, is seen as an aspect of the mind that identifies with the body and personal history, creating a sense of individuality and separation. This separation is considered an illusion that obscures the true self, or Atman, which is eternal, unchanging, and one with the ultimate reality, Brahman.

The spiritual practices in Hinduism, including Yoga and Vedanta, aim at dissolving the ego to realize the true self. This realization, known as Moksha or liberation, is achieved when one transcends the ego and recognizes one's inherent unity with all existence. Key to this is the practice of self-inquiry, as epitomized by the question "Who am I?", which seeks to peel away the layers of the ego to reveal the true self beneath.

## Taoism and the Ego: The Way of Naturalness

Taoism, the ancient Chinese philosophical and spiritual tradition, approaches the ego through the concept of Wu Wei, which translates to 'non-action' or 'effortless action'. This concept does not imply inaction but acting in harmony with the Tao, the fundamental principle that underlies and unifies all things in the universe.

In Taoist thought, the ego is seen as a source of disharmony and imbalance. It represents the unnecessary striving and artificial desires that disturb the natural flow of life. Taoism advocates for letting go of the ego and its forced efforts, encouraging a state of naturalness and simplicity where actions are in sync with the rhythm of the Tao. This alignment leads to a life of balance, spontaneity, and peace.

## Christian Mysticism: The Ego and Union with the Divine

In Christian Mysticism, the ego is often viewed as the barrier to experiencing a union with God. Mystics such as St. John of the Cross and Meister Eckhart spoke of the need to transcend the ego, or the false self, to realize the true self in God. This process, often described as a 'dark night of the soul', involves a deep purification where the ego with its attachments and desires is stripped away, leading to a profound spiritual awakening.

This tradition emphasizes the surrender of the ego to the divine will. Through this surrender and loss of the self, one gains a greater, more expansive identity in the sacred, experiencing a deep sense of unity and oneness with God.

## Sufism: Ego and the Journey to the Heart

Sufism, the mystical branch of Islam, views the ego, or Nafs, as the lower self that is driven by base desires and egotistical tendencies. The journey of a Sufi involves the purification of the Nafs through spiritual practices, devotion, and the guidance of a teacher. This purification process, often described as a journey from the Nafs to the heart, leads to a state where the ego is transcended, and the heart becomes the center of spiritual consciousness.

In Sufism, the transcendence of the ego is seen as essential to experiencing true love and knowledge of God. The ego is considered a veil that obscures the light of divine reality. Its transcendence leads to a state of selflessness, where the individual is immersed in the divine presence.

In summary, the concept of the ego in spiritual traditions is rich and multifaceted. While each tradition approaches it differently, common themes emerge – the ego as a source of illusion and separation, and its transcendence as a path to deeper understanding, unity, and liberation. These teachings offer invaluable perspectives for anyone seeking to understand the nature of the self and the potential for spiritual growth beyond the confines of the ego. Exploring the ego in these traditions is an intellectual exercise and a guide to a more awakened, harmonious, and profound way of living.

# The Ego Unfolded: Its Everyday Manifestations and Influence on Relationships and Self-Perception

In the intricate dance of daily life, the ego plays a central, often unacknowledged, role. This complex construct, deeply intertwined with our consciousness, shapes how we perceive ourselves and interact with the world around us. The ego, often misunderstood as merely a symbol of arrogance or pride, is far more nuanced. It encompasses our sense of identity, our self-esteem, and the multifaceted ways we present ourselves in various contexts. This article aims to dissect the manifestations of the ego in everyday life and explore its profound influence on our relationships and self-perception.

At its core, the ego serves as our psychological identity, a narrative we construct about who we are. This narrative is based on many factors, including our personal experiences, societal influences, cultural background, and aspirations. Through this narrative, we interpret our experiences, form our worldview, and engage with others. In its healthy form, the ego is essential; it helps us navigate the complexities of social interactions and make decisions that align with our values and beliefs. It gives us a sense of continuity and coherence in our life story.

However, the ego can also be a source of conflict and distortion. One of the most prominent ways the ego manifests in everyday life is through our constant pursuit of validation and recognition. This pursuit often stems from a deep-seated need to affirm our self-worth. Whether it's through social media likes, career achievements, or even the pursuit of physical attractiveness, these endeavours can be traced back to the ego's need for external validation. While seeking acknowledgement is natural, an overreliance on external validation can lead to a fragile sense of self heavily dependent on others' perceptions and approvals.

In personal relationships, the ego often manifests as a desire to maintain a certain image or be correct. It can lead to conflicts when the need to assert one's opinion or to defend one's self-image overshadows the importance of understanding and empathizing with the other person. In romantic relationships, ego-driven behaviours can manifest as jealousy, possessiveness, or a lack of compromise, often stemming from insecurities or a fear of vulnerability. In friendships, it can lead to competitiveness or a lack of authenticity, as individuals might hide their true selves in favour of a more favourable image.

Moreover, the ego significantly influences how we deal with criticism and failure. A robust and rigid ego may perceive criticism as a threat, leading to defensiveness or denial. This reaction can hinder personal growth, preventing us from seeing and addressing our flaws and mistakes. In the face of failure, an unbalanced ego might lead to excessive self-criticism or, conversely, to projecting blame onto others, thereby avoiding accountability.

The workplace is another arena where the ego's influence is readily apparent. The professional environment often triggers the ego's drive for status and recognition. While a healthy level of ambition can be constructive, an overinflated ego can lead to toxic competition, manipulation, and unethical behaviours. It can also impact leadership styles; leaders with unchecked egos may become authoritarian or narcissistic, while those with a more balanced ego might lean towards inclusivity and empathy.

Conversely, the ego also plays a crucial role in our self-perception and confidence. A well-balanced ego contributes to a healthy level of self-esteem, enabling us to set boundaries, assert our needs, and confidently pursue our goals. It helps us develop resilience, allowing us to bounce back from setbacks and maintain a positive self-image despite external challenges.

One of the most transformative approaches to dealing with the ego involves mindfulness and self-awareness practices. By becoming more aware of our thoughts, emotions, and behaviours, we can understand how our ego operates and influences our lives. This understanding enables us to respond to situations more consciously rather than reacting impulsively from our ego-driven patterns.

Additionally, meditation, journaling, and cognitive-behavioural techniques can help identify and modify ego-driven thoughts and beliefs. These practices foster a sense of inner peace and self-acceptance, reducing the ego's need for external validation and control.

With its multifaceted manifestations, the ego plays a significant role in shaping our daily experiences, relationships, and self-perception. While it is an essential component of our psychological makeup, an unexamined ego can lead to conflicts, distortions, and a disconnection from our authentic selves. By cultivating self-awareness and balance, we can harness the positive aspects of the ego while mitigating its negative influences. This balanced approach enables us to build healthier relationships, develop a more robust sense of self, and navigate the complexities of life with greater ease and authenticity.

# Taming the Ego: Exercises and Meditations for Self-Discovery

In the journey of self-awareness and personal growth, recognizing and observing the ego plays a crucial role. The ego, often misunderstood as just a sense of pride or self-importance, is a complex construct that shapes our perception, actions, and interactions. To understand and manage the ego is to pave the way for a more balanced, harmonious, and authentic life. This article introduces a series of exercises and meditations designed to help readers not only recognize and observe their ego but also understand its influence on their daily lives. These practices, rooted in various psychological and spiritual traditions, are tools for more profound self-discovery and transformation.

### Mindfulness: The Art of Observing the Ego

Mindfulness, a practice rooted in Buddhist meditation, is one of the most effective tools for observing the ego. Mindfulness involves paying attention to the present moment and observing thoughts, feelings, and sensations without judgment. This practice allows us to notice how the ego operates in real time. By becoming mindful, we can observe how the ego colours our perceptions, often leading us to react based on past conditioning or future anxieties.

A straightforward mindfulness exercise is to sit quietly and observe your thoughts for a few minutes each day. As you observe, note how many of your thoughts are centred around "I," "me," or "my." These thoughts might be worries about the future, past memories, judgments about others, or perceptions of how others see you. The objective is not to stop these thoughts but to notice them. This practice heightens awareness of the ego's presence and its habitual patterns.

## Journaling: Unveiling the Ego Through Writing

Journaling is another powerful tool for ego observation. Writing about daily experiences can help unearth the ego's narratives and beliefs. A helpful exercise is to write about a recent conflict or a stressful event, focusing on your thoughts and feelings during the incident. As you write, try to identify moments where your ego may have influenced your reactions. Were your actions driven by a need to be right, a fear of being perceived in a certain way, or a desire for control? Recognizing these ego-driven motives can be enlightening, helping to understand and gradually alter these ingrained patterns.

## The Mirror Exercise: Confronting the Ego

The mirror exercise, often used in psychological and spiritual practices, involves standing in front of a mirror and observing oneself. As you look at your reflection, notice the thoughts and judgments that arise. How much of your self-perception is tied to external appearances, and how does this affect your sense of self-worth? This exercise is not about criticizing or changing these thoughts but about becoming aware of how the ego shapes self-image and self-esteem.

## Body Scan Meditation: Sensing the Ego in the Body

A body scan meditation can be a revealing way to sense the ego's presence in the physical body. In this practice, focus your attention gradually on different body parts, observing any sensations or tensions. Emotional states linked to the ego, such as stress or defensiveness, often manifest as physical tightness. By becoming aware of these physical sensations, you can connect them with ego-driven emotions and thoughts, fostering a deeper mind-body awareness.

## Gratitude Practice: Diminishing the Ego's Hold

Cultivating gratitude is a gentle yet powerful way to diminish the ego's hold. The ego often focuses on what is lacking, leading to dissatisfaction and constant striving. By practicing gratitude, we shift our focus to what we have, fostering contentment and reducing the ego's constant craving for more. A daily gratitude practice, where you list things you are grateful for, can shift perspective from ego-driven desires to a more balanced and appreciative state of mind.

## Mindful Listening: Ego in Communication

Mindful listening exercises can be particularly practical in recognizing the ego in communication. During conversations, practice listening with full attention resisting the urge to formulate responses while the other person is speaking. Notice when the ego wants to interrupt, defend, or divert the conversation to your own experiences. Mindful listening fosters empathy and understanding, qualities often overshadowed by the ego's need to dominate or be heard.

## Reflection on Ego-Driven Behaviours

Reflecting on instances where ego-driven behaviours manifested can be illuminating. Think of times when you felt offended, angered, or hurt. Often, these emotions are tied to the ego feeling threatened or diminished. Reflecting on these instances and considering alternative, less ego-centric responses can help understand the ego's triggers and develop more constructive responses.

## Letting Go Visualization

Visualization exercises can also help in loosening the ego's grip. Imagine placing your ego-centric thoughts, beliefs, and attachments in a balloon and releasing it. As you watch it float away, observe the feelings that arise. This visualization symbolizes the release of the ego's hold and can be a powerful symbolic practice for cultivating detachment.

Understanding and managing the ego is not about suppression or elimination but about recognizing its patterns and learning to balance its influence. These exercises and meditations offer a path to greater self-awareness, fostering a relationship with the ego that is observant but not beholden. Through these practices, we can cultivate a sense of inner peace, improved relationships, and a more authentic way of being, moving beyond the ego's illusions to a fuller expression of our true selves.

# Chapter 5: The Weight of Grudges and Resentment

The human heart, complex and profound in its depth, often becomes the repository of intense emotions, among which grudges and resentments loom large. These emotions, deeply rooted in our experiences of hurt and betrayal, can become chronic burdens, silently affecting our emotional, spiritual, and even physical well-being.

Grudges and resentments are often the result of unresolved conflicts, perceived injustices, and deep-seated hurt. They arise when we feel wronged or slighted by others —through words, actions, or neglect. While the initial emotional response is natural and even justified, the problem arises when these feelings persist, turning into lingering resentments and grudges. Holding onto these feelings can be likened to carrying an invisible weight that gradually, yet inevitably, wears down our spirit and zest for life.

One of the most significant impacts of harbouring grudges is the emotional toll it takes. Prolonged feelings of anger, bitterness, or desire for revenge can lead to constant emotional turmoil. This inner unrest can seep into various aspects of life, affecting our mood, attitude, and ability to enjoy life's pleasures. The emotional strain is not just a fleeting state; it can manifest in chronic stress, anxiety, and depression, deeply affecting our mental health and quality of life.

The spiritual consequences of holding onto grudges are equally profound. Many spiritual traditions advocate for forgiveness and letting go of resentments as essential pathways to inner peace and enlightenment. Holding grudges can be seen as a form of spiritual self-imprisonment, where one is shackled by past hurts and unable to move forward. In spiritual terms, releasing these negative emotions is akin to setting the soul free, allowing it to rise to higher levels of understanding and compassion.

Moreover, the physical impact of long-term resentment and grudges is increasingly recognized in medical research. The stress and negative emotions associated with these feelings can lead to physiological changes in the body, such as increased blood pressure, weakened immune system, and heightened risk of heart diseases. The old adage that holding onto anger is like drinking poison and expecting the other person to die rings with a certain literal truth in the light of these findings.

Forgiveness is often proposed as the antidote to the poison of grudges. However, forgiveness is not a straightforward process. It is a complex emotional journey involving understanding, empathy, and a conscious decision to relinquish the desire for retribution. Forgiveness does not necessarily mean forgetting the hurt or reconciling with the wrongdoer. Instead, it is about freeing oneself from resentment, allowing healing and moving on with life.

This chapter also delves into practical steps and techniques for releasing resentment and forgiving. These include mindfulness practices, which help recognise and accept one's feelings without being overwhelmed. Journaling can be another effective tool, providing a safe space to express and reflect emotions. There are also specific forgiveness exercises and meditations designed to facilitate letting go.

Additionally, understanding the psychology behind why people hold grudges can be enlightening. Personality traits, upbringing, and past experiences play a significant role in dealing with hurt and betrayal. Some may find it easier to forgive and move on, while others might struggle with letting go of resentment. Recognizing these personal factors can be crucial in addressing and overcoming grudges.

The chapter also explores the role of empathy in the process of forgiveness. Developing empathy towards the person who has wronged us can be a challenging yet powerful step in overcoming grudges. Trying to see the situation from the other person's perspective, understanding their motivations, and acknowledging their humanity can shift the dynamic from anger to compassion.

In conclusion, "The Weight of Grudges and Resentment" offers an understanding of these heavy emotional burdens and practical ways to lift them. This exploration aims to guide readers towards emotional healing, spiritual growth, and a more peaceful and contented life. Letting go of grudges and embracing forgiveness is not just about improving our relationships with others; it is fundamentally about healing and liberating ourselves.

## Unraveling the Tangled Web

Grudges and resentment are complex emotional states that can profoundly impact our mental health and interpersonal relationships. Rooted deeply in the human psyche, these feelings are more than just temporary reactions to perceived wrongs; they are intricate psychological processes influenced by various factors. To understand why individuals hold onto grudges and resentment, it's essential to delve into the psychological underpinnings that govern these emotions. This exploration sheds light on personality traits, past experiences, and various psychological theories, offering insights into why letting go of negative emotions can be so challenging for some.

Grudges and resentment typically arise when an individual feels wronged or hurt. This could be due to actual harm caused by another person or a perceived injustice or betrayal. What makes these emotions particularly enduring is how they are processed and internalized. Unlike fleeting anger or disappointment, grudges involve a persistent rumination over the incident and an ongoing sense of injustice or hurt. This rumination can become a mental habit, where the individual repeatedly replays the offending scenario, reinforcing negative emotions and attitudes.

One key factor in understanding the psychology of grudges is personality traits. Certain personality types are more prone to holding grudges. For instance, individuals with a propensity for neuroticism – a trait characterized by a tendency towards negative emotional states – may be more likely to grab onto grudges due to their heightened sensitivity to perceived slights or hurts. On the other hand, people with high levels of agreeableness may be more inclined to forgive and move on, valuing harmony and positive relationships over nursing past wounds.

Past experiences also play a significant role in shaping an individual's propensity to hold grudges. Early life experiences, particularly those involving trust and betrayal, can set the stage for how individuals deal with hurt and disappointment in later life. For example, someone who experienced betrayal or inconsistent treatment in childhood may develop a defensive mechanism of holding grudges to protect themselves from future hurts. These early experiences can create deeply ingrained patterns of behaviour and reaction, making it difficult to break the cycle of resentment.

Psychological theories offer additional insights into why some people struggle to overcome grudges. Cognitive theory suggests that our thoughts and beliefs about a situation can influence our emotional responses. Suppose an individual believes that they were wronged in an unforgivable way or that their grudge is justified as a form of self-protection. In that case, these beliefs can perpetuate feelings of resentment. Similarly, behavioural theories highlight the role of learned behaviours. If holding a grudge has been a known response to conflict or hurt, it can become an automatic reaction over time.

Another perspective comes from evolutionary psychology, which suggests that the tendency to hold grudges could have had adaptive benefits in early human societies. Bearing a grudge could serve as a social tool to signal to others that unjust actions have consequences, thereby deterring future harm. While such mechanisms may have been beneficial in ancestral environments, prolonged grudges can lead to strained relationships and emotional distress in modern society.

The difficulty in releasing grudges and resentment can also be understood through emotional processing. Letting go often requires confronting painful emotions and acknowledging vulnerability, which can be daunting. There can be a fear that forgiving or releasing the grudge might lead to further emotional pain or vulnerability to future harm. Additionally, for some, a grudge can become part of their identity – a story about themselves and their experiences that they hold onto, even if it causes them pain.

The psychology behind grudges and resentment is multifaceted, involving a complex interplay of personality traits, past experiences, cognitive and behavioural patterns, and even evolutionary factors. Understanding these underpinnings is crucial in addressing and overcoming these negative emotions. It involves recognizing the patterns of thought and behaviour that sustain grudges, processing the feelings tied to them, and, ultimately, finding ways to let go and move forward. This process is not only beneficial for personal well-being but also for fostering healthier and more positive relationships.

# The Hidden Toll

Holding onto grudges, a common human experience, is like carrying a silent burden. While it may seem like a justified response to hurt and betrayal, clinging to these negative emotions can significantly affect an individual's emotional and spiritual well-being. This exploration delves into how nurturing grudges impacts our lives, often in ways that are not immediately apparent. It illuminates the complex interplay between our emotional responses and more profound spiritual health, revealing why letting go is beneficial and essential for our holistic well-being.

The emotional response to being wronged is at the heart of holding a grudge. When we perceive that someone has harmed us, whether through their actions or words, it triggers a cascade of emotions, including anger, hurt, and a sense of injustice. Initially, these emotions are natural and even necessary, as they signal that something significant has occurred that requires our attention and possibly our defence. However, when these feelings solidify into a grudge, they create enduring emotional unrest.

The emotional toll of holding onto grudges is multi-layered. On the surface, there is the persistent negative emotion – the anger or hurt that resurfaces each time we recall the incident. This repeated activation of negative emotions can lead to chronic stress. This state is known to have various adverse effects on mental health, including anxiety, depression, and a general decrease in emotional well-being. Chronic stress can also manifest physically, contributing to issues such as hypertension, digestive disorders, and a weakened immune system.

Beneath this layer of immediate emotional response, there is a deeper impact on the individual's emotional health. Holding onto grudges can lead to a pervasive sense of bitterness and cynicism. Over time, this can color an individual's worldview, leading to a more negative outlook on life and relationships. It can create a defensive stance towards the world, where trust diminishes and new relationships are approached with caution, if not outright suspicion. This stance can lead to isolation and a sense of disconnection, further exacerbating unhappiness and dissatisfaction.

On a spiritual level, the impact of harbouring grudges is profound. Many spiritual traditions emphasize the importance of forgiveness and letting go of resentments as key to spiritual growth and enlightenment. From this perspective, holding onto grudges is a barrier to spiritual development. It anchors the individual in past hurts, preventing them from fully engaging with the present and moving forward in their spiritual journey. In many traditions, spirituality is closely linked with qualities of compassion, love, and openness. Grudges, inherently tied to anger and closed-heartedness, are antithetical to these spiritual qualities.

Furthermore, nurturing grudges often leads to an inner conflict that can impact one's sense of peace and harmony. This conflict arises because holding onto negative emotions towards someone else inevitably involves a certain degree of self-negation. It requires maintaining a state of emotional agitation and unease, contrary to the human drive towards happiness and peace. This dissonance can create a feeling of being emotionally and spiritually stuck, hindering personal growth and fulfilment .

In addition to the personal toll, holding grudges can also ripple effect on one's social and relational environment. It can strain existing relationships, especially if the grudge also impacts those around the individual. For instance, family or mutual friends may feel divided or pressured to take sides. Furthermore, the negative energy of a grudge can be palpable, creating an atmosphere of tension and hostility that affects others.

Another aspect to consider is the energy and time spent maintaining a grudge. Nurturing resentment requires a considerable amount of psychological effort. This effort and its emotional energy could be redirected towards more positive and constructive pursuits. The persistence of a grudge can, therefore, lead to a significant opportunity cost, robbing the individual of potential joy, creativity, and productive engagement with life.

The journey towards releasing grudges involves emotional work and reorientating one's spiritual outlook. It requires acknowledging and processing the hurt, understanding the dynamics that led to the grudge, and consciously letting go of the resentment. This process often involves cultivating empathy and compassion for oneself and the person who caused the hurt. It may also involve spiritual practices such as meditation, prayer, or rituals that symbolize forgiveness and release.

The emotional and spiritual toll of holding onto grudges is a complex and multi-faceted issue that significantly impacts an individual's quality of life. While letting go of grudges is challenging, especially when the hurt is deep, it is a crucial step towards emotional healing, spiritual growth, and overall well-being. Releasing resentment and cultivating forgiveness is not just about improving one's relationship with others; it is fundamentally about healing and freeing oneself. Individuals can embark on greater peace, fulfilment, and spiritual harmony by understanding the profound costs of nurturing grudges and taking active steps to release them.

## Embracing Forgiveness

Forgiveness stands out as a powerful and transformative tool in the complex tapestry of human emotions. Often misunderstood and sometimes viewed as a sign of weakness, forgiveness, in reality, is a profound act of strength and self-compassion. It is a deliberate choice, a journey towards healing, not just for those who have been wronged but also for the ones who choose to forgive. This article explores the multifaceted role of forgiveness in letting go of grudges and resentment, its healing power, and the profound impact it can have on an individual's life and well-being.

Forgiveness is often misconceived as a simplistic act of forgetting or excusing hurtful actions. However, at its core, forgiveness is about releasing the grip of negative emotions tied to past events. It's a conscious decision to let go of anger, bitterness, and the desire for revenge – feelings that, while initially natural, can become toxic over time. This process of letting go does not necessarily mean reconciliation or condoning the harmful actions. Instead, it's about finding peace, reclaiming personal power, and moving forward.

The journey towards forgiveness often begins with acknowledging and processing the hurt. This step is crucial and involves allowing oneself to feel and understand the emotions that the hurtful event triggered. It is about permitting oneself to grieve the injustice or betrayal. This acknowledgement is not an act of indulgence in victimhood but a necessary phase for emotional healing. By confronting these emotions, individuals can disentangle themselves from the pain and the past event.

Understanding the nature of forgiveness is essential in this healing journey. Forgiveness is not a one-time act but a process. It might require revisiting the emotions and the decision to forgive multiple times. Each time, the emotional hold of the past hurt lessens, making way for more peace and less pain.

One of the most significant challenges in forgiving is overcoming the ego's resistance. The ego, tied to our sense of identity and self-preservation, often holds onto grudges as protection. It builds a narrative around the hurt, reinforcing a sense of righteousness and victimhood. Breaking free from this narrative requires a deep understanding that holding onto resentment harms oneself more than it affects the perpetrator.

The benefits of forgiveness extend beyond emotional relief. Numerous studies have shown that forgiveness can have significant health benefits. These include lowering the risk of heart attack, improving cholesterol levels, reducing pain, blood pressure, levels of anxiety, depression, and stress. This physical aspect of forgiveness underscores the deep connection between emotional well-being and physical health.

Forgiveness also opens the door to spiritual growth and understanding. Many spiritual traditions advocate forgiveness as a path to enlightenment and inner peace. From a spiritual perspective, forgiveness is a release from the karmic ties to the person who caused the hurt. It's a step towards evolving spiritually, transcending the ego, and connecting with a higher sense of purpose and compassion.

Practising forgiveness, however, does not come easily. It often requires a combination of introspection, empathy, and sometimes even professional help. Empathy plays a crucial role in the process. Understanding the circumstances or reasons behind the perpetrator's actions can provide a different perspective. This understanding does not justify the hurtful actions but can lessen the personal sting and facilitate the letting go.

In addition to empathy, various psychological and spiritual practices can aid in forgiveness. These include mindfulness meditation, which helps gain control over runaway thoughts and emotions; journaling, which provides a means to express and work through feelings; and counselling or therapy, which offers guided support in navigating the complexities of forgiveness.

Forgiveness also involves a reclamation of power. It is a shift from a passive experience where one is acted upon, to an active choice where one decides how to respond to the hurt. This shift is empowering. It transforms the narrative from one of a victim to that of a survivor, a person who is capable of overcoming pain and choosing peace and well-being.

Forgiveness is a potent tool for healing and personal growth. It allows individuals to break free from the chains of past hurts and to reclaim their emotional and spiritual well-being. The journey of forgiveness is deeply personal and often challenging, but it is also liberating and transformative. Embracing forgiveness is embracing a life of peace, health, and fulfilment, moving beyond the pain and limitations of the past into a more hopeful and empowered future.

# Finding Freedom

Resentment, a deep-seated feeling of anger or bitterness as a result of unfair treatment, can be a consuming force, impacting mental health, relationships, and overall quality of life. While it's a familiar and understandable reaction to hurtful situations, lingering resentment can become a heavy burden. The key to emotional freedom often lies in releasing these feelings. This article explores practical steps and techniques to help individuals break free from resentment, foster healing, and restore peace.

The first step in releasing resentment is the acknowledgement of the emotion itself. It involves recognizing and accepting that you are harbouring these feelings without judgment. People may often try to suppress resentment due to guilt or a perception that such feelings are unjustified or inappropriate. However, acknowledging is crucial because releasing what you haven't admitted to holding is impossible. This step doesn't mean dwelling on the negative emotions, but rather allowing yourself to see them clearly and understand them as a natural response to your experiences.

Once acknowledged, the next step is to express these feelings constructively. Bottled-up resentment can lead to emotional and physical distress, so finding safe and healthy ways to communicate these emotions is vital. Journaling can be a powerful tool for this. Writing about your feelings of resentment and the events that triggered them can help clarify your thoughts and emotions. For some, speaking to a trusted friend, family member, or therapist can provide a similar outlet. The key is to express these feelings in a way that doesn't harm yourself or others.

Another effective technique in the journey of releasing resentment is the practice of empathy and perspective-taking. This involves trying to understand the situation from the other person's point of view. It's not about excusing their behaviour but about recognizing that there may be factors you are unaware of that influenced their actions. Empathy doesn't justify the hurt caused but can diffuse the intensity of resentment by adding a new dimension of understanding to the situation.

Additionally, practicing mindfulness and meditation can be extremely helpful in managing the emotions associated with resentment. Mindfulness involves staying present and engaged with your current experiences without judgment. You can learn to observe your resentment without getting caught up in it through mindfulness. Meditation, especially loving-kindness meditation, can also be beneficial. This practice involves sending feelings of kindness and goodwill first to yourself and then to others, including those who have wronged you. This doesn't mean you condone their actions but wish for peace and healing for everyone involved.

One of the most challenging yet crucial steps in releasing resentment is making a conscious decision to forgive. Forgiveness is often misunderstood as a sign of weakness or as giving in. In reality, it's a powerful act of self-care. Forgiving doesn't mean you forget the incident or that you are okay with what happened. Rather, it means you choose to let go of resentment's hold on you. This decision might need to be made repeatedly, as old feelings can resurface over time.

Reframing the experience that led to resentment can also be a transformative technique. This involves shifting the focus from your victimization to what you have learned or how you have grown from the experience. It might include recognizing strengths you didn't know you had, empathy you've developed, or a deeper understanding of your own boundaries and values. This shift doesn't negate the pain or unfairness of the situation but allows you to derive something positive from it.

Incorporating self-compassion into your daily routine is another key step. Resentment often coexists with harsh self-judgment. Practicing self-compassion involves treating yourself with the same kindness and understanding you would offer a good friend in a similar situation. It means acknowledging that suffering, failure, and imperfection are part of the shared human experience.

Finally, engage in activities that foster positivity and well-being. These could be hobbies, exercise, leisure time in nature, or connecting with loved ones. These activities can help shift your focus away from past hurts and towards things that bring you joy and fulfilment .

Releasing resentment is not an instantaneous or easy process. It requires time, patience, and a commitment to self-reflection and personal growth. You can gradually lift the weight of resentment by acknowledging and expressing your feelings, practicing empathy and forgiveness, and focusing on self-care and positivity. This journey leads to emotional healing and greater inner peace and freedom.

# *Chapter 6: Embracing Impermanence and Change*

In the grand tapestry of human existence, change is the only constant. Yet, for many, the concept of impermanence is a source of deep unease and discomfort. The natural human inclination is to seek stability, predictability, and permanence. However, in its intrinsic nature, life flows like a river - ever-changing, ever-evolving.

The idea of impermanence has been a central theme in numerous spiritual teachings and philosophies throughout history. In Buddhism, the recognition of impermanence, or Anicca, is fundamental. It posits that all of existence, including our thoughts, feelings, and physical world, is constantly in flux. This realization is pivotal to the Buddhist understanding of life and the path to enlightenment. Similarly, in Hinduism, the material world, or Maya, is seen as transient, urging seekers to look beyond the temporary to the eternal. Taoist philosophy also embraces the ever-changing nature of reality, encouraging alignment with the natural flow of life, which is dynamic and ever-transforming.

Yet, understanding and accepting impermanence is more than a spiritual exercise; it has profound implications for our daily lives and mental well-being. Accepting change can be a powerful antidote to the suffering caused by clinging to attachments and the rigid constructs of the ego. When we acknowledge that nothing is permanent, we can begin to release our grasp on the material, the external, and the illusion of control. This acceptance opens the door to a more flexible, adaptable approach to life, where change is not something to be feared but embraced as an opportunity for growth and renewal.

This chapter delves into how embracing impermanence can transform our experiences of loss, transition, and uncertainty. It explores the liberation that comes from understanding that change is inevitable and intrinsic to the human condition. Through this lens, the end of a relationship, the loss of a job, or even the passing of a loved one can be viewed as part of life's natural ebb and flow, rather than as unbearable catastrophes.

Personal narratives and anecdotes shared in this chapter will illustrate the profound impact of embracing impermanence and change. These stories will offer a window into the lives of individuals who have navigated significant transitions, weathered losses, and emerged with a deeper understanding and acceptance of life's transitory nature. These accounts will serve as beacons of inspiration and guidance for readers navigating their paths through the unpredictable waters of life.

Furthermore, the chapter will provide practical advice and strategies for cultivating a mindset that embraces change. It will offer tools and exercises to help readers develop resilience in the face of life's uncertainties and find peace and contentment amid change. From mindfulness practices to cognitive reframing techniques, readers will be equipped with a toolkit for navigating change with acceptance and a sense of empowerment and grace.

This chapter is an invitation to embark on a transformative journey. It encourages readers to shift their perspective from viewing change as a threat to recognizing it as an integral, enriching part of the human experience. By embracing the impermanent nature of life, we open ourselves to a deeper appreciation of the present, a more fluid and adaptive approach to life's challenges, and a path to true inner freedom.

## Impermanence in Spirituality

Impermanence, a concept deeply ingrained in various spiritual teachings, presents a fundamental truth about the nature of existence: everything is constantly in flux. This article explores how different spiritual traditions understand and interpret impermanence and how this understanding shapes their worldview and practices. By delving into this concept, we gain insights into the transient nature of life, which can be both a source of existential anxiety and profound liberation.

In Buddhism, the concept of impermanence, or Anicca, is integral. It asserts that all of existence is transient, in constant change, and without permanent essence. The Buddha taught that life is like a river – ever-flowing, ever-changing. This understanding is crucial to Buddhist thought, as it underpins the nature of suffering (Dukkha) and the path to liberation (Nirvana). According to Buddhist teachings, suffering arises from our desire to hold onto things that are, by nature, impermanent – whether they are physical objects, relationships, or even our emotions and thoughts. The realization of Anicca reduces clinging and attachment, paving the way for inner peace and enlightenment.

Hinduism, with its rich tapestry of philosophies and practices, also contemplates the transient nature of the world. In Hindu thought, the physical world (Maya) is seen as an illusion, a play of the divine, constantly changing and impermanent. This perception encourages a detachment from the material world and a focus on the eternal soul (Atman) and the ultimate reality (Brahman). The Bhagavad Gita, a key Hindu scripture, teaches that wise are those who remain unperturbed by change, understanding that just as the body sheds worn-out clothes for new ones, the soul moves on from old to new states of existence.

Taoism, an ancient Chinese philosophy and spiritual practice, views impermanence as a fundamental characteristic of the Tao (the Way). The Tao Te Ching, a foundational text of Taoism, speaks of the ever-changing nature of life, urging adherence to the flow of the natural world. It advocates for a life of simplicity and flexibility, where one is in harmony with the cycles of change rather than resisting them. Adherents find tranquility amid life's constant flux by aligning with the Tao.

In Western spiritual traditions, impermanence is also a recurring theme, though often approached from different angles. Christianity, for example, while focusing on the eternal nature of the soul and the afterlife, also acknowledges the transient nature of earthly life. Biblical teachings often remind believers of the fleeting nature of human existence and the futility of clinging to material possessions. This recognition is meant to steer focus towards spiritual pursuits and the eternal life beyond the physical realm.

The concept of impermanence has profound psychological implications. It challenges our natural tendency to seek security and permanence in an inherently unstable and ever-changing world. This clash between our desires and the world's reality can be a source of significant distress. However, spiritual teachings argue that there is freedom in accepting impermanence. When we embrace the transient nature of everything, we are more likely to appreciate the present moment, reduce our anxieties about the future, and find peace in the knowledge that change is the essence of life.

Moreover, accepting impermanence often leads to a greater sense of compassion and connectedness. Recognizing that everyone is subject to the same laws of change fosters a sense of shared humanity. It can lead to more empathetic relationships, as we understand that just like us, others are also navigating the uncertainties of life.

In practice, many spiritual traditions offer techniques and practices to help internalize the concept of impermanence. Meditation, mindfulness, contemplative prayer, and reflective rituals are standard methods used to deepen the understanding and acceptance of life's transitory nature. These practices help individuals cultivate a more adaptable, resilient mindset, and open to the flow of life.

The concept of impermanence is a cornerstone in many spiritual teachings. It provides a lens through which we can view the ever-changing nature of our lives and the world around us. While recognising impermanence can initially be unsettling, it ultimately offers a pathway to deeper understanding, acceptance, and peace. Embracing this transient nature of existence allows us to live more fully in the present, appreciate the fleeting beauty of life, and find a more profound sense of connection with the world and our fellow beings.

## The Liberation in Change

In the intricate journey of life, one of the most profound challenges and sources of growth is the acceptance of change. Constant and inevitable change often confronts the rigid structures of our attachments and the walls of our ego. This article explores how accepting change is a passive resignation and an active process that can lead to significant emotional and spiritual liberation. By understanding and embracing the dynamic nature of life, we can release the grip of attachments and the constraints of the ego, paving the way for a more authentic and fulfilling existence.

At the core of many personal struggles is the resistance to change. This resistance is often rooted in the natural human desire for stability and predictability. Attachments, whether to people, possessions, beliefs, or even our self-image, provide a sense of security and continuity. However, when these attachments become too rigid, they can lead to suffering, especially in the face of life's inevitable changes. Similarly, with its desire to maintain a consistent and favorable self-identity, the ego often struggles against the transformative tides of change.

Accepting change begins with recognising that change is life's very fabric. Everything, from the smallest cells in our body to the vastest galaxies, is in constant flux. This impermanent nature of the universe means that attachment to any fixed state is futile and often a source of pain. When we understand this, we can start to loosen our emotional and mental grip on things, people, and ideas, opening ourselves to the flow of life.

The process of releasing attachments is deeply intertwined with the diminishing of the ego. The ego, which thrives on certainty and control, finds change threatening. It builds identities and stories that are resistant to alteration. Accepting change means challenging these stories and identities. It requires us to question who we are and what we value beyond the rigid confines of our ego-driven narratives.

One of the transformative aspects of accepting change is the cultivation of flexibility and resilience. When we stop expending energy on resisting change, we can redirect this energy towards adapting and growing. This adaptability is not about losing our sense of self, but about finding a self more in tune with the realities of life. It's about developing a sense of robust yet flexible identity, capable of withstanding life's fluctuations without breaking.

Accepting change also fosters a deeper sense of presence and appreciation. When we acknowledge the transitory nature of life, we begin to appreciate the present moment more fully. This heightened presence can lead to a richer, more vibrant life experience. It allows us to cherish our relationships, experiences, and possessions without clinging to them. We learn to love and enjoy without the fear and pain of loss overshadowing our experiences.

Moreover, accepting change is often accompanied by a profound sense of freedom. The energy that was once used to resist change or to maintain attachments and uphold the ego can now be utilised for personal growth and exploration. This freedom is not just an absence of constraints but a positive presence of new possibilities. It opens doors to new experiences, relationships, and ways of being that were previously obscured by our attachments and ego.

The journey towards accepting change often involves introspective practices such as meditation, mindfulness, and reflective journaling. These practices help develop an awareness of our attachments and the workings of our ego. They also cultivate the mental and emotional space needed to observe change without reacting immediately. This space is crucial for making conscious choices rather than being driven by unconscious patterns of attachment and ego.

Additionally, embracing change can lead to greater empathy and compassion. As we understand and experience the transient nature of our own lives, we can relate more deeply to the experiences of others. This shared human condition of impermanence can become a source of connection rather than isolation, fostering a sense of community and understanding.

The path of accepting change is not linear or easy. It is fraught with challenges and setbacks. However, each step on this path can be enriching, each challenge an opportunity to learn and grow. By embracing the impermanent nature of life, letting go of our attachments, and understanding the role of the ego, we embark on a journey towards a more liberated and authentic existence. This journey enables us to live fully, love deeply, and face the vicissitudes of life with grace and courage.

## Navigating Life's Tides

Major life transitions, whether anticipated or unexpected, can be some of the most defining moments in our journey. These periods of change —the loss of a loved one, a shift in career, or a personal transformation — test our resilience and adaptability. Often, they require us to re-evaluate our identity, values, and the very fabric of our daily lives. This article delves into the challenges of significant life changes. It offers insights and strategies for navigating these transitions with grace and resilience, highlighting how accepting impermanence is a source of strength and renewal.

Regardless of their nature, life transitions typically involve a period of ending, followed by a phase of uncertainty and ambiguity, and eventually, a new beginning. This cycle is evident in nature and human life alike. It's essential to recognize that transitions are not just about the physical changes that occur but also about the psychological and emotional adjustments we must make in response to these changes.

The initial phase of a significant life transition often involves a sense of loss. This could be the loss of a job, a relationship, a loved one, or even an aspect of self-identity. Such losses can trigger a grieving process, which may include denial, anger, bargaining, depression, and acceptance. These stages are not linear and can vary greatly in duration and intensity from person to person.

A key to navigating life transitions is embracing the impermanence of life. This concept, central to many spiritual and philosophical teachings, reminds us that change is the only constant. By acknowledging that everything in life is transient, we can reduce our resistance to change and open ourselves to transformation.

Accepting impermanence allows us to appreciate the present moment, even amidst uncertainty fully. It encourages us to let go of our attachment to specific outcomes and to embrace the journey of change with an open mind and heart. This perspective can transform our experience of transitions from something we endure to something we actively engage with and learn from.

Strategies for Navigating Transitions

> **Acknowledging and Expressing Emotions**: Major life changes often evoke strong emotions. It's crucial to acknowledge these feelings rather than suppress them. Journaling, talking to a trusted friend or therapist, or engaging in creative expression can provide outlets for these emotions.

> **Seeking Support**: Transition periods can feel isolating but don't have to be navigated alone. Seeking support from

friends, family, support groups, or professional counselors can provide comfort and guidance. Shared experiences and perspectives can offer validation and new coping strategies.

**Establishing Routines and Self-Care Practices**: During times of change, maintaining some routine can provide a sense of stability. Additionally, prioritizing self-care through activities like exercise, meditation, or hobbies can enhance well-being and provide much-needed respite.

**Setting Realistic Expectations and Goals**: Transitions are processes, and setting realistic expectations and goals is important. This might mean acknowledging that feeling settled or achieving new objectives will take time, and that's okay.

**Focusing on Learning and Growth**: Viewing transitions as opportunities for learning and growth can shift our perspective from loss to potential gain. Reflecting on what can be learned from these experiences can provide a sense of purpose and direction.

**Practicing Flexibility and Openness**: Being open to new experiences and flexible in our approaches can significantly ease the transition process. It allows us to explore new possibilities and readily adapt to changing circumstances.

**Cultivating Gratitude**: Even in times of change, there can be aspects of life to be grateful for. Focusing on these can shift our attention from what we have lost to what we still have or are gaining.

**Exploring Spirituality or Philosophical Beliefs**: Many find strength and comfort in exploring their spiritual or philosophical viewpoints. These can provide a framework for understanding and navigating life's changes.

**Setting Boundaries**: Recognizing and communicating our limits during transitions is essential. Setting boundaries around our time, energy, and emotional capacity can help manage stress and maintain relationships.

**Visualizing the Future**: Engaging in visualization exercises where you imagine a positive future can be a powerful tool for maintaining hope and motivation. It helps create a mental image of what life could look like post-transition.

# *Chapter 7: The Path to Inner Peace and Fulfilment*

In the relentless pursuit of happiness and contentment, individuals often navigate a complex labyrinth of emotions, experiences, and aspirations. The quest for inner peace and fulfilment is as ancient as humanity itself, yet it remains an elusive goal for many. This chapter, "The Path to Inner Peace and Fulfilment ," is an expedition into the heart of this timeless quest. It aims to demystify the journey towards achieving a serene mind and a contented life, delving into practices that transcend material possessions and the ego, and exploring the roles of mindfulness, meditation, self-awareness, and more in nurturing a fulfilled and peaceful existence.

Misconceptions often cloud the pursuit of inner peace and fulfilment . In a world that frequently equates happiness with material success and external achievements, there's a tendency to overlook the profound depths of internal well-being. This pursuit is not about acquiring more possessions or attaining high status but is instead an inward journey. It is about discovering a sense of peace and contentment that is not contingent on external circumstances but rooted in a deep understanding and acceptance of oneself and the world.

Central to this journey is the concept of detaching from material possessions and the ego. While possessions and a healthy sense of self are essential aspects of life, undue attachment to them can lead to a perpetual state of desire and dissatisfaction. Cultivating inner peace involves learning to find joy and contentment beyond these attachments. It's about understanding that true fulfilment comes from within and that the external world, while enjoyable and necessary, is not the ultimate source of happiness.

Mindfulness, a practice with its roots in ancient spiritual traditions and now validated by modern psychology, is a cornerstone of this journey. Mindfulness is the art of being fully present in the moment, of engaging with life here and now, without judgment or distraction. This practice allows individuals to break free from the mind's constant chatter, the endless rumination over past regrets, and anxiety about the future. By fostering a state of mindful awareness, one can experience life more fully, appreciate the simple joys, and handle challenges with a calmer, more balanced approach.

Similarly, meditation, a practice as diverse as it is ancient, is a powerful tool in the quest for inner peace. Meditation offers a pathway to quiet the mind, reduce stress, and connect with deeper aspects of the self. It provides a space for introspection and can bring profound insights into one's thoughts, emotions, and underlying beliefs. Through regular meditation, individuals can cultivate a sense of inner tranquillity that permeates all aspects of their life.

Self-awareness, too, plays a critical role in this journey. It involves deeply understanding one's personality, emotions, motivations, and reactions. Self-awareness is about observing oneself objectively, recognizing strengths and acknowledging areas for growth. This self-knowledge is essential for personal development and for fostering relationships that are based on authenticity and mutual respect.

However, the path to inner peace and fulfilment is not just about individual practices but also how one interacts with the world. This includes the cultivation of gratitude and positive thinking, balancing personal goals with inner values, and building healthy relationships and community connections. Gratitude and positive thinking shift the focus from lacking to abundance, fostering a sense of contentment. Balancing personal ambitions with internal well-being ensures that one's pursuits are aligned with their deeper values. Building and maintaining healthy relationships and engaging in community life provides a sense of connection and belonging, which are fundamental to human happiness.

This chapter also recognizes the unique challenges of modern life. Finding inner peace can seem more challenging than ever in an era characterized by constant connectivity, relentless demands, and a pervasive sense of competition. Yet, in these challenges, the value of inner tranquillity becomes most apparent. The practices and principles discussed in this chapter counterbalance contemporary life's frenetic pace, providing tools and perspectives to navigate the modern world with a sense of calm and purpose.

Furthermore, the chapter offers practical guidance on integrating these practices into daily life. From simple mindfulness exercises that can be incorporated into routine activities, to meditation practices suited for different lifestyles, and strategies for developing self-awareness, the chapter provides actionable steps for anyone looking to embark on this path. It also includes narratives and anecdotes that bring these concepts to life, illustrating how individuals from various walks of life have walked this path and found a sense of peace and fulfilment.

The journey to inner peace and fulfilment is deeply personal, infinitely varied, and often challenging. Yet, it is also gratifying. This chapter serves as a guide, a companion on this journey, offering insights, practices, and encouragement. It is an invitation to explore the depths of your being, discover a wellspring of peace and contentment, and live a life marked by a sense of purpose, joy, and serenity.

## Beyond the Material

In the quest for a fulfilling and peaceful life, many find themselves entangled in pursuing material possessions and the bolstering of ego. However, true contentment often lies beyond these tangible acquisitions and self-centric viewpoints. Inner peace and fulfilment stem from a deeper place within, rooted in practices that transcend life's material and egoistic facets. This article explores a range of practices that nurture this profound sense of well-being, offering guidance on cultivating a life rich in peace and satisfaction that is not solely dependent on external factors.

The foundation of finding inner peace and fulfilment often starts with the realization that material possessions, while providing temporary comfort and pleasure, do not equate to lasting happiness. Similarly, with its endless demands for recognition and validation, the ego often leads to an unfulfilling cycle of desire and competition. The practices discussed here aim to shift focus from these external dependencies to more enduring sources of contentment.

Mindfulness and meditation are powerful practices for cultivating inner peace. They involve focusing the mind on the present moment and observing thoughts, feelings, and sensations without judgment. This practice helps detach from the mind's constant chatter and the influence of the ego, bringing about a state of calm and clarity. Meditation, in its various forms, allows individuals to delve deeper into their inner world, fostering a sense of tranquillity and self-awareness. Regular practice can profoundly transform how one experiences life, perceives challenges and interacts with others.

Self-awareness is a critical aspect of achieving inner peace and fulfilment. It involves understanding one's thoughts, emotions, and behaviours. This understanding enables individuals to recognize patterns that may be disruptive or unhelpful, such as habitual reactions driven by the ego or undue attachment to material possessions. Developing self-awareness can be facilitated through practices like journaling, reflective thinking, and psychotherapy. These practices encourage introspection and a deeper understanding of one's motivations and desires.

Gratitude is a simple yet profound practice. It involves focusing on and appreciating what one has rather than fixating on what is lacking. This shift in perspective can significantly alter one's life experience, fostering a sense of abundance and contentment. Practices to cultivate gratitude include maintaining a gratitude journal, where one regularly notes things they are thankful for, and mindfulness exercises that focus on appreciating the present moment.

Embracing simplicity and minimalism can be a powerful antidote to the constant pursuit of more possessions, achievements, and stimuli. This approach involves paring down life to its essentials, finding joy and satisfaction in simplicity, and reducing dependence on material possessions. Minimalism isn't about deprivation; rather, it's about creating space for what truly matters. This space allows for more freedom, less clutter (both physical and mental), and an environment that supports inner peace.

Engaging in charitable activities, such as volunteering, community service, or simple acts of kindness, can significantly enhance one's sense of fulfilment and connection to others. These activities shift the focus from the self to the well-being of others, reducing the influence of the ego and fostering a sense of interconnectedness. Altruism has been linked to increased happiness, decreased stress, and a greater sense of purpose.

While solitude is essential for introspection and self-connection, meaningful social connections are equally important for emotional well-being. Balancing time alone with time spent in the company of others is crucial. Solitude allows for reflection and personal growth, while healthy relationships provide support, joy, and a sense of belonging. Cultivating this balance involves setting aside time for self-reflection and nurturing supportive and enriching relationships.

Life is unpredictable, and change is inevitable. Adopting a flexible mindset helps you easily navigate life's ups and downs. This includes letting go of rigid expectations, adapting to new situations, and viewing challenges as opportunities for growth. A flexible mindset reduces the resistance to change, often a source of stress and unhappiness.

Spending time in nature can have a calming and rejuvenating effect, offering a respite from modern life's fast-paced, material-focused aspects. Connecting with nature can involve hiking, gardening, or simply spending time in a park. This connection often brings a sense of peace and a reminder of the natural rhythms of life, which are larger and more enduring than individual concerns and desires.

Physical health is deeply intertwined with mental and emotional well-being. Regular exercise, a balanced diet, and adequate rest are fundamental in maintaining the physical vitality needed to pursue inner peace and fulfilment. Physical health practices also offer a way to channel energies positively, reduce stress, and enhance mood.

Many find that exploring spiritual or philosophical paths provides insights and guidance on the journey to inner peace. This exploration can involve studying spiritual texts, engaging in spiritual practices, or simply contemplating life's more significant questions. It often leads to a deeper understanding of oneself and the world, offering perspectives that transcend material and ego-centric views.

The integration of these practices into daily life is key to their effectiveness. This integration can be gradual, starting with small, manageable changes and building upon them. It might involve setting aside specific times for meditation or journaling, incorporating moments of gratitude into the day, or consciously making choices that align with a more minimalist and simplicity-focused lifestyle.

Navigating life's path to inner peace and fulfilment is a profoundly personal and ever-evolving journey. It requires patience, commitment, and a willingness to explore and experiment with different practices. The journey is not always linear or smooth but invariably enriching. By shifting focus from external dependencies to internal sources of peace and contentment, individuals can discover a wellspring of profound and enduring fulfilment. This path, though unique to each person, offers a universal invitation to explore the depths of our being and to live a life marked by tranquillity, satisfaction, and a sense of true accomplishment.

## Mindfulness, Meditation, and Self-Awareness

Embarking on the journey to inner peace and fulfilment often involves delving deep into the realms of the self, navigating through layers of consciousness and unconsciousness. At the heart of this introspective journey lie three crucial practices: mindfulness, meditation, and self-awareness. These practices are more than mere techniques; they are transformative processes that guide individuals towards a greater understanding of their inner world, leading to profound peace and fulfilment. This article explores the intricate roles of mindfulness, meditation, and self-awareness in this journey, shedding light on how these practices interweave to create a tapestry of internal harmony and self-discovery.

Mindfulness is a practice rooted in ancient Buddhist teachings, yet it resonates profoundly with the contemporary search for peace and fulfilment. It involves being fully present in the moment, paying attention to our thoughts, feelings, bodily sensations, and the environment around us, without judgment or distraction. The practice of mindfulness is about cultivating a state of open, non-judgmental awareness, where each moment is observed and experienced fully, whether it is pleasant, unpleasant, or neutral.

The power of mindfulness lies in its simplicity and its profound impact on our everyday lives. It helps in breaking the automaticity of habitual reactions, thoughts, and behaviours. By becoming more aware of our moment-to-moment experiences, we can start to recognize patterns in our thoughts and emotions, particularly those that lead to stress, anxiety, or unhappiness. Mindfulness teaches us to respond to life's challenges with clarity and calmness rather than reacting impulsively or out of emotion-fueled reflex.

Incorporating mindfulness into daily life can take many forms, from structured practices like mindfulness meditation to informal practices like mindful eating, walking, or listening. The essence of mindfulness is the same regardless of the method – it's about paying attention to the present moment with acceptance and curiosity.

While mindfulness is about being present in all aspects of life, meditation provides a structured way to hone this skill. Meditation, in its various forms, is a practice of focused attention or contemplation to achieve mental clarity, emotional calmness, and heightened awareness. It is a cornerstone in the pursuit of inner peace and fulfilment, offering a retreat from the noise and demands of the external world.

The benefits of meditation are vast and well-documented. Regular meditation practice has been shown to reduce stress, anxiety, and depression, improve concentration and memory, and enhance overall well-being. On a deeper level, meditation enables individuals to connect with their inner selves, fostering a sense of peace and contentment that transcends external circumstances.

Different meditation techniques cater to different needs and preferences. These include concentration meditation, where focus is maintained on a single point or object; mindfulness meditation, which involves observing thoughts and sensations without attachment; and loving-kindness meditation, aimed at cultivating feelings of compassion and love for oneself and others.

Self-awareness is intimately linked with mindfulness and meditation. It involves a conscious understanding and insight into one's character, feelings, motives, and desires. This self-knowledge is crucial in the journey to inner peace and fulfilment as it lays the foundation for personal growth and self-improvement.

Self-awareness allows individuals to understand their emotional triggers, strengths, weaknesses, and behaviour patterns. It provides a basis for making changes and choices that are aligned with one's true self and values. Self-awareness also fosters a deeper understanding of how our internal states affect our interactions with others and our world perception.

Practices to enhance self-awareness include reflective journaling, therapy or counseling, and mindfulness techniques that encourage observation and analysis of one's thoughts and feelings. Cultivating self-awareness is often challenging, as it can reveal uncomfortable truths about ourselves, but it is essential for true inner growth and happiness.

Integrating mindfulness, meditation, and self-awareness into daily life is a personal and evolving process. It can begin with small steps, such as setting aside a few minutes daily for meditation or practicing mindful breathing during stressful moments. The key is consistency and a willingness to explore and experiment with different practices to find what resonates most.

Mindfulness, meditation, and self-awareness are not quick fixes but lifelong practices that enrich and deepen over time. They require patience, dedication, and an open heart. As these practices become more integrated into one's life, they gradually transform how we experience ourselves and the world, leading to greater peace, clarity, and fulfilment .

In essence, the journey to inner peace and fulfilment is coming home to oneself. It's about discovering the tranquility and joy that reside within, beyond the transient allure of material possessions and the fleeting satisfactions of the ego. Mindfulness, meditation, and self-awareness guide this journey, offering paths to a life of greater presence, purpose, and peace. Through these practices, we learn to navigate life's complexities with balance and grace, finding contentment and fulfilment within ourselves, irrespective of external circumstances.

## Weaving Mindfulness and Self-Awareness into the Fabric of Everyday Life

Integrating mindfulness, meditation, and self-awareness into daily life is a transformative journey that can significantly enhance one's sense of peace and fulfilment . However, making these practices a part of our everyday routine often seems challenging amidst the hustle and bustle of modern life. This article offers practical guidance on weaving these essential practices into the fabric of daily living, ensuring they become not just activities we do, but part of who we are.

The journey begins with understanding the value these practices add to our lives. Mindfulness, the art of being fully present and engaged with the here and now, offers a way to live life more fully, with greater appreciation and less stress. Meditation provides a space for inner exploration and tranquillity, helping us find calm and clarity amid life's chaos. Self-awareness enables us to understand ourselves better, leading to more authentic and fulfilling relationships with ourselves and others. Appreciating these benefits is the first step in committing to these practices.

One of the simplest ways to integrate mindfulness into daily life is to start small and anchor it in routine activities. Mindful eating, for example, is a practice that can be commenced immediately. It involves paying full attention to the eating experience, noticing the food's flavors, textures, and sensations, and the process of eating itself. This practice enhances the enjoyment of meals and encourages a healthier and more conscious approach to dining.

Mindful walking is another accessible practice. This involves being fully present during walks, whether it's a short stroll to a nearby store or a longer walk for exercise. It's about feeling the ground beneath your feet, noticing the rhythm of your steps, the sensation of the air on your skin, and the sights and sounds around you. This practice transforms a routine activity into an opportunity for mindfulness.

Incorporating meditation into daily life can start with dedicating just a few minutes each day to the practice. It doesn't require hours of sitting; even five to ten minutes can make a significant difference. The key is consistency. Finding a regular time and place for meditation helps establish it as a habit. This could be in the morning to start the day with a sense of calm, or in the evening, to unwind and reflect. Guided meditations available through apps or online can be helpful for beginners.

Self-awareness practices can be integrated into daily routines through regular self-reflection. This can be done through journaling, where you spend a few minutes each day writing down your thoughts, feelings, and experiences. This practice helps recognise patterns in thoughts and behaviours, understand emotional triggers, and make conscious decisions.

Another aspect of integrating these practices is to create mindfulness reminders. These cues in your environment or daily schedule prompt you to pause and return to the present moment. For instance, setting a reminder on your phone to take deep breaths or to check in with your current thoughts and emotions can be effective.

Mindfulness, meditation, and self-awareness can also be integrated through mindful communication. This involves being fully present in conversations, listening actively, and speaking authentically. It means paying attention to the words and tone of voice, body language, and underlying emotions, both in yourself and the other person.

In addition to individual practices, finding a community or group that shares your interest in these practices can be highly beneficial. Community support provides motivation, learning opportunities, and a sense of belonging. Whether it's a meditation group, a mindfulness workshop, or an online community, connecting with others can enrich the practice and encourage.

The workplace is another arena where mindfulness and self-awareness can be integrated. Simple practices like taking short mindfulness breaks to reset and refocus, using deep breathing techniques to manage stress, or adopting mindful listening during meetings can significantly enhance work experience and effectiveness.

A crucial part of integrating these practices is being patient and kind to yourself. Change doesn't happen overnight, and there will be days when you're more successful in your practice than others. It's important to approach this as a journey with its ups and downs, rather than a destination with a fixed endpoint.

Finally, integrating mindfulness, meditation, and self-awareness into daily life is about making these practices a part of your lifestyle. It's about finding joy and allowing these practices to evolve and adapt to your changing needs and circumstances. Over time, these practices become not just something you do, but a way of being, deeply ingrained in the way you live your life.

Through consistent practice and integration into daily activities, mindfulness, meditation, and self-awareness can transform your life experience. They open up a world where each moment is lived fully, challenges are met with clarity and calm, and life is navigated with an underlying sense of peace and purpose. The path to integrating these practices is as unique as the individual walking it, filled with discoveries and insights that enrich the journey towards inner peace and fulfilment.

# *Chapter 8: Transforming Relationships through Letting Go*

In the intricate dance of human relationships, the steps are often complicated by the burdens we carry - our egos, attachments, past hurts, and unspoken expectations. Though deeply personal, these invisible loads do not just weigh us down individually; they also impact the quality and nature of our interactions with others.

At the heart of many relationship challenges lies the ego - that part of us that craves recognition, validation, and supremacy. In its desire to protect and elevate the self, the ego often becomes a wall separating us from others. It can manifest in various forms: the need to always be right, the fear of vulnerability, or the drive to control. Similarly, our attachments – to ideas, beliefs, or a particular way of being – can create expectations that bind and restrict not just ourselves but also those we relate to. These attachments can lead to disappointment, resentment, and conflict when reality does not align with our tightly held-expectations.

Letting go in relationships involves a conscious effort to release the grip of the ego and our attachments. It requires a willingness to examine our patterns, question our motives, and embrace vulnerability. This journey is not about losing ourselves or giving up on what matters to us; rather, it's about gaining a deeper, more compassionate understanding of ourselves and others. It's about recognizing that we find the space for true connection and harmony in the fluidity of letting go.

One of the most transformative aspects of letting go is cultivating empathy and understanding. By loosening the hold of our ego and attachments, we open ourselves to truly seeing and hearing others. We become more receptive to different perspectives, experiences, and emotions. This receptivity enriches our relationships, fostering a climate of mutual respect and understanding.

Forgiveness, both of ourselves and others, is a vital component of letting go. Holding onto past grievances or mistakes often serves as a barrier to moving forward in relationships. Forgiveness does not mean condoning hurtful actions or forgetting the pain caused. Instead, it is an act of freeing oneself from the bitterness and resentment that hinders emotional growth and the deepening of relationships. It is about making peace with the past to create a more hopeful and positive future.

Transforming relationships by letting go also redefining our understanding of strength and control. Contrary to the common perception, there is immense strength in vulnerability and openness. It takes courage to express our true feelings, admit our mistakes, and show our authentic selves. Similarly, letting go of the need to control outcomes or other people leads to greater inner peace and allows relationships to flourish in their natural rhythm and course.

Real-life examples and stories of relationships that have been healed and enriched by letting go provide both inspiration and practical insights. These narratives, drawn from various contexts – be it family, friendships, romantic partnerships, or workplace interactions – illustrate the profound impact of embracing vulnerability, empathy, and forgiveness. They highlight how, through letting go, relationships can evolve into more meaningful, satisfying, and supportive experiences.

In addition to personal anecdotes, this chapter also explores various techniques and practices that facilitate letting go in relationships. These include mindfulness exercises that enhance present-moment awareness and reduce reactive patterns, communication strategies that foster openness and authenticity, and reflective practices such as journaling, which provide insights into one's thoughts and feelings.

Integrating the practice of letting go into relationships is not an overnight transformation. It is a gradual process filled with learning, unlearning, trials, and triumphs. It involves becoming aware of when our ego and attachments dictate our interactions and consciously choosing a different path of openness, understanding, and compassion.

Furthermore, the chapter discusses navigating the challenges and resistances that often arise on this path. Letting go, especially in deeply entrenched relationships, can be met with fear, uncertainty, and even resistance from others. Navigating these challenges requires patience, perseverance, and a deep commitment to personal growth and relational harmony.

Transforming relationships through letting go is about finding freedom from the patterns and behaviours that limit us and our relationships. It's about creating relationships that are rooted in authenticity, respect, and genuine connection. This transformation is not just about improving our interactions with others but also about evolving into our best selves - more aware, compassionate, and connected to the richness of human experience.

This chapter is more than just a guide; it is a journey into the heart of what makes our relationships complex, challenging, and incredibly rewarding. It invites readers to embark on a path of self-discovery and relational renewal, promising a destination where relationships are not just endured but are sources of joy, growth, and deep fulfilment. Through the art of letting go, we unlock the potential for our relationships to become conduits of love, understanding, and lasting peace.

## Forgiveness as a Cornerstone of Relationship Healing and Renewal

In personal and professional relationships, forgiveness is often touted as a key to healing and growth. Yet, its true depth and complexity are seldom fully appreciated. Forgiveness is not just a moral virtue or a fleeting gesture of reconciliation; it is an intricate psychological process that plays a crucial role in the dynamics of relationships. This article delves into the nature of forgiveness, its challenges, and its profound impact on healing and strengthening relationships. It also distinguishes between the concepts of forgiving and forgetting and outlines steps towards genuine forgiveness, offering valuable insights for those seeking to mend and nurture their relationships.

Forgiveness in its essence, is the process of letting go of resentment, anger, and thoughts of revenge that stem from a perceived wrong. It's about moving past the hurt and negative feelings associated with an offense, whether it's a minor slight or a significant betrayal. However, it's important to note that forgiveness does not necessarily mean condoning the wrong action, minimizing one's pain, or reinstating trust immediately. It's a personal journey that primarily benefits the one who forgives.

The psychological and emotional process of forgiving starts with acknowledgment – recognizing that there has been hurt and pain. This acknowledgment is crucial as it validates the emotions involved and allows the process of healing to begin. The next step involves understanding, where one tries to see the situation from a broader perspective. This might include considering the offender's circumstances, possible intentions, or their own struggles. It doesn't justify the action but provides a context that might make forgiveness feel more accessible.

Emotionally, forgiveness involves a shift from holding onto anger and resentment to gradually releasing these feelings. This shift doesn't happen overnight and is often a gradual process of letting go of the emotional burden. It's about consciously choosing to leave behind the negativity associated with the offense and deliberately deciding to move forward.

The challenges in the path of forgiveness are manifold. The most significant challenge is the emotional intensity associated with the hurt. Deep-seated hurt and betrayal can create strong resistance to forgiveness. In some cases, there might be a feeling that forgiving is equivalent to giving the offender a 'free pass' or that it undermines the gravity of the offense. Another challenge is the misconception about what forgiveness entails – it is often confused with reconciliation or forgetting the offense, which is not always the case.

The distinction between forgiving and forgetting is critical. Forgiving is about releasing the hold of negative emotions and thoughts related to the offense, while forgetting is about erasing the memory of the incident. Forgiveness does not imply forgetting; rather, it's about remembering differently – without the emotional pain and resentment. It's about learning from the experience and moving on, rather than erasing it from memory.

Genuine forgiveness involves several key steps. The first step is self-reflection, where one acknowledges their feelings and the offence's impact on their life. The second step is the expression of these feelings in a safe environment, which could be through talking to a trusted friend, journaling, or even directly communicating with the offender, if appropriate. The third step is the decision to forgive — a conscious choice to release the feelings of resentment and anger. This decision is often followed by a period of emotional work, where one gradually lets go of negative emotions and cultivates positive feelings like empathy, compassion, or understanding.

Integrating forgiveness into relationships requires patience and practice. It often helps to start with smaller grievances before tackling more significant issues. Setting boundaries is also important — forgiveness does not mean allowing the harmful behaviour to continue. Sometimes, professional help in the form of counseling or therapy may be needed, especially when dealing with deep-seated hurts or complex relationship dynamics.

Forgiveness can lead to profound healing and strengthening of relationships. It opens the door to better communication, deeper understanding, and renewed trust. Professional relationships can foster a more cooperative and positive work environment. Personal relationships can deepen the bond and create a stronger foundation for future interactions.

In the journey of relationships, forgiveness stands as a beacon of hope and renewal. It's a path that leads to the healing of past wounds and the opening of new possibilities for growth and connection. By embracing forgiveness, individuals can transform their relationships, moving from conflict and resentment to understanding, peace, and fulfilment . Forgiveness, therefore, is not just an act of mercy towards the other but a gift of liberation to oneself.

## Bridging Hearts and Minds

Effective communication is a vital bridge between hearts and minds in the intricate web of human relationships. The foundations of strong, healthy relationships are built through the exchange of words, emotions, and understanding. Particularly when addressing the challenge of resentment - a common and corrosive emotion in personal and professional relationships - the role of communication becomes paramount. This article explores practical communication strategies that aid in releasing resentment and building understanding, thereby fostering empathy and healing in relationships. By examining ways to express feelings constructively, the importance of active listening, and the power of compassionate communication, we can uncover pathways to dissolve misunderstandings and conflicts, paving the way for more fulfilling connections.

Effective communication of one's feelings and needs is fundamental in managing and resolving resentment. The first step in this process is self-reflection, which involves identifying and understanding one's emotions and their reasons. Once this clarity is achieved, it becomes easier to express these feelings to others in a direct yet non-confrontational way.

One effective technique for expressing feelings is the use of "I" statements. This approach focuses on how you feel rather than what the other person has done wrong, reducing the likelihood of the conversation escalating into a blame game. For instance, saying "I feel hurt when I am not included in decisions" is less likely to provoke defensiveness than "You never include me in decisions." This method of expression allows for openness and vulnerability, inviting empathy rather than conflict.

Another important aspect of communicating feelings is being specific about the issue. Vague accusations or generalizations can lead to confusion and defensiveness. It is more effective to pinpoint exact instances or behaviours that led to the feelings of resentment. This specificity clarifies the message and provides a concrete basis for addressing the issue.

Active listening is a critical component of effective communication, especially when resentment is present. It involves fully concentrating on what is being said, rather than just passively 'hearing' the speaker's message. Active listening requires the listener to be fully present, acknowledging the speaker's feelings, and responding thoughtfully. It is an act of empathy that can transform the dynamics of a conversation.

One way to practice active listening is to paraphrase what the speaker has said, which shows that you are truly engaged and understand their perspective. Asking open-ended questions to clarify points or to delve deeper into the speaker's feelings can also be beneficial. Active listening demonstrates respect and care for the speaker's feelings and experiences, which can be a powerful antidote to resentment.

Open and compassionate communication is the cornerstone of resolving conflicts and overcoming resentment. This type of communication is characterized by honesty, empathy, and a genuine desire to understand the other person's perspective. It involves not only expressing one's own feelings and needs but also being receptive to the feelings and needs of others.

Practising compassionate communication often requires us to put aside our ego and our desire to be right. It involves approaching conversations with a mindset of finding solutions and understanding rather than winning an argument. This approach fosters a safe environment where all parties can express their feelings without fear of judgment or reprisal.

When emotions are running high, it is also important to know when to take a break from the conversation. Taking a moment to cool down can prevent the situation from escalating and can lead to more productive discussions.

Integrating these communication strategies into daily interactions requires practice and mindfulness. It can be helpful to start by applying these techniques in less charged situations before employing them in more emotionally intense conversations. Regular practice can make these strategies more natural and effective when handling difficult discussions.

Another important aspect is to set the right tone for the conversation. Approaching discussions with a calm and open demeanour sets a positive precedent. Choosing the right time and setting for important conversations is also beneficial, ensuring that all parties are comfortable and willing to engage.

Additionally, it is essential to acknowledge that effective communication is a two-way street. While you can control how you communicate, you cannot control how others respond. Patience and persistence are key, as is the willingness to seek external help, such as mediation or counseling, when necessary.

Effective communication is a powerful tool in healing relationships and overcoming resentment. We can build bridges of understanding and empathy by learning to express our feelings constructively, listening actively, and communicating with openness and compassion. These bridges help resolve current conflicts and lay the groundwork for more robust, more resilient relationships in the future. Through conscious communication, we can transform our interactions, turning points of contention into opportunities for growth and deeper connection.

# Chapter 9: Integrating Letting Go into Everyday Life

In our fast-paced, achievement-oriented world, the concept of letting go and embracing a lifestyle of non-attachment and humility can seem counterintuitive and counterproductive. We are often taught that more is better – more success, possessions, and control. However, this relentless pursuit often leads to stress, dissatisfaction, and a perpetual feeling of chasing something elusive. Chapter 9, "Integrating Letting Go into Everyday Life," invites readers on a transformative journey, exploring how letting go and embracing humility can enrich our lives, bring peace, and lead to lasting fulfilment. This chapter is not just a guide but an invitation to a different way of living and being, offering practical advice, discussing the challenges and rewards, and providing daily exercises to assist in this profound journey.

Letting go, rooted in various spiritual and philosophical traditions, is fundamentally about releasing our tight grip on life – our need to control, possess, and attach to people, outcomes, and material possessions. It's a shift from a mindset of scarcity and possession to one of abundance and freedom. This shift, however, is not about renouncing the world or its pleasures; it's about finding a balance where we can engage with the world fully, yet not be consumed by our attachments to it.

Living a life of non-attachment and humility is often misunderstood. It does not mean indifference or lack of ambition. Rather, it's about cultivating a state of mind where one's sense of well-being is not overly dependent on external circumstances. It's about learning to value experiences over possessions, relationships over accolades, and personal growth over societal approval. This lifestyle advocates for a deep appreciation and engagement with life, but with a detachment that allows for a sense of peace and contentment, regardless of the external situation.

The challenges of adopting this way of life, especially in contemporary society, are significant. The constant barrage of materialistic messaging, societal pressures to conform to certain standards of success, and the innate human fear of loss and change can all act as barriers. Overcoming these challenges requires not just understanding but a deep, sustained commitment to practice and self-reflection. It's a journey that involves unlearning some of the deeply ingrained beliefs and patterns of behaviour that society has instilled in us.

The rewards of this lifestyle, however, are profound. Letting go can lead to a reduction in stress and anxiety, as the need to control every aspect of life diminishes. It can foster more muscular, authentic relationships, as interactions are no longer driven by ego and possessiveness. Non-attachment can also lead to greater freedom and liberation, as one's happiness is no longer contingent on external achievements or possessions. Humility, in turn, can foster a deeper sense of connection with others and the world, as it allows for empathy, understanding, and a recognition of our shared human experience.

Incorporating the principles of non-attachment and humility into daily life is not about making dramatic changes overnight. It's about small, consistent steps that gradually transform the way we view and interact with the world. Daily exercises and rituals play a crucial role in this. They can range from mindfulness practices that help stay present and reduce attachment to outcomes, to gratitude exercises that shift focus from what we lack to what we have, to acts of kindness and service that reinforce humility and connection with others.

One effective practice is mindfulness meditation, which focuses on the present moment and observes thoughts and feelings without attachment or judgment. This practice helps in recognizing and releasing unhealthy attachments and patterns of thought. Another exercise is the practice of gratitude, where one regularly reflects on and appreciates the simple joys and blessings in life. This practice can counteract the tendency always to want more, fostering a sense of contentment and appreciation for what is.

Journaling is another powerful tool. Writing about experiences, especially challenging ones, can provide insights into how attachments and ego may influence thoughts and behaviours. It can also be a space to reflect on moments of letting go and the feelings associated with them.

Integrating these practices into daily life also involves being mindful of our interactions and responses. It's about pausing before reacting, considering whether actions are driven by ego or attachment, and consciously choosing responses that reflect non-attachment and humility.

Another aspect is redefining our relationship with material possessions. This doesn't necessarily mean living a minimalist lifestyle, though for some, that might be their chosen path. It's more about evaluating our relationship with our possessions and understanding whether they bring genuine value and joy or if they are merely symbols of status or success.

Balancing ambition with non-attachment is another area of focus. It involves setting goals and striving to achieve them, but doing so with an awareness that self-worth is not solely dependent on outcomes. It's about finding joy in the process and learning from successes and failures.

Navigating relationships through the lens of non-attachment and humility can be particularly challenging yet deeply rewarding. It involves learning to appreciate and love others while respecting their autonomy and freedom. It's about building relationships based on mutual respect, understanding, and genuine connection rather than possessiveness, control, or dependency.

Integrating letting go into everyday life is a journey towards inner peace and fulfilment. It's a path that leads to a deeper understanding of oneself and the world, fostering a rich life not in possessions but in experiences, relationships, and a sense of contentment that endures regardless of external circumstances. This chapter guides embarking on this transformative journey, providing the tools, insights, and encouragement to explore a liberating, fulfilling, and deeply enriching way of living.

# Embracing Simplicity and Humility

In a world that often equates success with accumulation and self-worth with achievement, choosing a path of non-attachment and humility can seem like a radical departure. However, this path offers a profound sense of freedom and fulfilment for those seeking deeper meaning and inner peace. Living a life of non-attachment and humility does not mean rejecting ambition or the joys of life. Instead, it involves redefining our relationship with our desires, possessions, and ego. This article provides practical advice on how to cultivate non-attachment and humility in daily life, offering steps to a more balanced, peaceful, and authentic existence.

The journey begins with understanding what non-attachment and humility truly mean. Non-attachment is often misunderstood as disinterest or detachment from the world. In reality, it is about engaging with life fully but without being enslaved by our desires and possessions. It means finding joy and fulfilment in experiences and relationships for their own sake, not for the status, power, or material gain they may bring.

Humility, on the other hand, is often mistaken for self-deprecation or weakness. True humility is about recognizing our own limitations and the value of others. It's an acknowledgement that we are part of a larger whole and that our achievements and failures are not solely the product of our efforts but the result of many factors, including the support and contributions of others.

Practical Steps to Cultivate Non-Attachment

> **Mindful Consumption**: Start by becoming more aware of your consumption habits. Ask yourself whether what you're buying or pursuing is necessary and what motivates your desire. Is it a need, a genuine source of joy, or an attempt to fill an emotional void? Mindful consumption helps in reducing attachment to material possessions.

> **Gratitude Practices**: Cultivate gratitude by regularly acknowledging and appreciating what you have. This could be through daily gratitude journaling or simply taking a moment each day to reflect on the things you're thankful for. Gratitude shifts focus from what we lack to the abundance present in our lives.

> **Simplify Your Life**: Simplifying your life can mean decluttering your physical space, reducing commitments that don't align with your values, or simplifying your daily

routines. This practice creates space in your life for what truly matters and reduces the stress of overcommitment and physical clutter.

**Mindfulness and Meditation**: Engage in mindfulness and meditation practices. These practices help cultivate an awareness of the present moment and an acceptance of what is, reducing the constant striving for more and the dissatisfaction with what is.

## Practical Steps to Foster Humility

**Self-Reflection**: Regular self-reflection is key to developing humility. Reflect on your strengths and weaknesses, recognize your achievements, and acknowledge the role others have played in your success. This helps in maintaining a balanced view of oneself.

**Listen More, Speak Less**: Make a conscious effort to listen more and speak less in your interactions. Listening fosters understanding respect for others' viewpoints, and reduces the urge to dominate conversations or impose your opinions.

**Serve Others**: Engage in acts of service without the expectation of recognition or reward. Service can range from formal volunteering to simple acts of kindness in daily life. Serving others fosters a sense of community and empathy, crucial components of humility.

**Seek Feedback**: Regularly seek feedback from friends, family, and colleagues. Feedback provides perspectives outside our own and can be a humbling experience that fosters personal growth.

## Challenges and Rewards

Living a life of non-attachment and humility is not without its challenges. It requires swimming against the current of a culture that often values the opposite. Letting go of long-held beliefs about success and self-worth can be difficult. However, the rewards are substantial. Non-attachment brings a sense of freedom, reducing the anxiety and stress associated with loss and change. It fosters resilience, as happiness becomes less dependent on external circumstances. Humility brings deeper relationships, as it allows for more genuine connections with others, free from the dynamics of competition and ego.

Daily Exercises and Rituals

**Daily Mindfulness Practice**: Dedicate a few minutes each day to mindfulness practice. This could be through meditation, mindful walking, or simply practicing awareness in daily activities like eating or listening.

**Regular Decluttering**: Make it a habit to declutter your physical and digital spaces regularly. This practice is a physical manifestation of letting go and can help in reducing attachment to possessions.

**Reflective Journaling**: Keep a reflective journal. Use it to explore your thoughts and feelings about attachment, achievements, and your interactions with others. This practice can provide insights into your inner world and foster self-awareness.

**Acts of Kindness**: Incorporate small acts of kindness into your daily routine. These acts can be as simple as helping a stranger or offering a listening ear to a friend. Such acts help in shifting focus from the self to others.

Integrating non-attachment and humility into everyday life is a gradual process that requires patience and persistence. It is a path of personal growth that enhances individual well-being and enriches interactions with others and the world. By embracing the principles of non-attachment and humility, we open ourselves to a life marked by deeper satisfaction, stronger relationships, and a profound sense of peace. It is a journey well worth undertaking, one that leads to a more meaningful, balanced, and joyful existence.

# Navigating Challenges and Embracing Rewards

Embarking on a lifestyle centered around non-attachment and humility presents a fascinating paradox. On one hand, it promises a serene and more meaningful existence, free from the relentless pursuit of material possessions and societal status. On the other, it poses significant challenges, testing our deeply ingrained beliefs and behaviours. This article delves into the intricate tapestry of this lifestyle, exploring the hurdles that one might encounter and the profound rewards that can be reaped from such a transformative journey.

Challenges of a Lifestyle of Non-Attachment and Humility

**Cultural and Social Pressures**: One of the most formidable challenges in embracing a life of non-attachment comes from societal norms and expectations. We live in a culture that often equates success with accumulation and self-worth with achievement. Stepping away from these norms to lead a life that prioritizes non-attachment can lead to misunderstandings, judgments, or even isolation from peers who may not share or understand your values.

**Internal Resistance and Ego**: The human ego is intricately tied to possessions, achievements, and recognition. Letting go of these can feel like a direct threat to our ego and identity. There's often an internal struggle, a resistance to letting go of what we have been conditioned to believe are markers of a successful life. This internal resistance can manifest as doubt, fear, and a sense of loss.

**Practical Challenges in Implementation**: Integrating the principles of non-attachment into everyday life can be practically challenging. It requires constant mindfulness and conscious decision-making, which can be draining, especially in the initial stages. The challenge is in consistently choosing actions and reactions that align with the principles of non-attachment and humility.

**Emotional Challenges**: Letting go, especially of deep-seated attachments and beliefs, can be an emotionally turbulent process. It may involve revisiting and releasing past hurts, forgiving oneself and others, and dealing with feelings of vulnerability from stepping away from the ego's protective shield.

## Rewards of a Lifestyle of Non-Attachment and Humility

Despite these challenges, the rewards of a lifestyle rooted in non-attachment and humility are profound and life-changing.

**Inner Peace and Contentment**: Perhaps the most significant reward is the attainment of a deep sense of inner peace and contentment. Non-attachment liberates from the constant need for more, reducing stress and anxiety associated with loss, change, and failure. It fosters an inner tranquility that remains stable regardless of external circumstances.

**Improved Relationships**: This lifestyle also paves the way for healthier, more authentic relationships. Humility allows for better understanding and empathy, reducing conflicts and enhancing connections. Non-attachment in relationships fosters a love that is free from conditions and possessiveness, leading to deeper, more meaningful interactions.

**Enhanced Self-Awareness and Personal Growth**: Living a life of non-attachment and humility accelerates personal growth and self-awareness. It encourages introspection, helping individuals to understand their true motives, desires, and values. This awareness is crucial for personal development and leads to more deliberate and fulfilling life choices.

**Resilience in the Face of Adversity**: Non-attachment builds resilience. By reducing dependency on external factors for happiness and self-worth, individuals become more adaptable and resilient in the face of life's ups and downs. They learn to navigate changes and challenges with greater ease and less turmoil.

**A Sense of Freedom**: There is an immense sense of freedom that comes with non-attachment. It is the freedom from the exhausting pursuit of keeping up, competing, and acquiring. This freedom opens up space for creativity, exploration, and engaging with life more relaxed and joyfully.

**Living with Purpose and Mindfulness**: This lifestyle encourages living with purpose and mindfulness. It fosters a conscious way of living, where each decision and action is aligned with one's deepest values and beliefs. This mindful way of living leads to a more present, vibrant, and engaged experience of life.

### Navigating the Journey

Navigating the journey towards non-attachment and humility requires patience, perseverance, and compassion towards oneself. It often involves redefining success and happiness, understanding that they are not dictated by external achievements but by the quality of one's inner life. It also means being open to learning and growing from the challenges, understanding that each hurdle provides an opportunity for deeper self-understanding and spiritual growth.

Support systems such as like-minded communities, spiritual or mindfulness practices, and sometimes professional guidance can be invaluable in this journey. They provide the necessary encouragement, perspective, and tools to navigate the challenges effectively.

Embracing a life of non-attachment and humility is a deeply personal and transformative journey. It challenges conventional beliefs and habits, but in doing so, it opens up a world of peace, contentment, and profound fulfilment . This path, while not without its trials, offers a unique and enriching way of experiencing life, relationships, and oneself. It is a journey that leads not just to a destination of inner peace but to a new way of being in the world — one that is freer, richer, and infinitely more rewarding.

# Daily Practices for Transformation

Embarking on a journey of letting go and embracing a life of non-attachment and humility requires more than just a philosophical understanding; it necessitates practical, daily actions that reinforce these concepts. Integrating specific exercises and rituals into one's daily routine can be profoundly transformative, aiding in the gradual shift from a life driven by attachment and ego to one of greater peace, simplicity, and fulfilment . This article offers a collection of practical exercises and rituals designed to assist readers on their journey toward letting go, providing a roadmap for daily practice that can lead to significant personal transformation.

## Mindfulness Meditation

A cornerstone of cultivating a lifestyle of letting go is the practice of mindfulness meditation. This form of meditation involves focusing on the present moment, acknowledging and accepting thoughts, feelings, and bodily sensations without judgment. Starting the day with just five to ten minutes of mindfulness meditation can set a tone of calm and centeredness for the hours ahead. It allows one to begin the day with a clear mind, grounded in the present, rather than being pulled by the regrets of yesterday or the worries of tomorrow.

## Gratitude Journaling

Another powerful daily practice is maintaining a gratitude journal. Each morning or evening, take a few minutes to write down three things you are grateful for. These can be as simple as a beautiful sunrise, a pleasant conversation, or a good cup of coffee. This practice shifts focus from what is lacking to the abundance already present in life, fostering a mindset of contentment and appreciation.

## Daily Reflection

Setting aside time each day for reflection is crucial in the journey of letting go. This could be a quiet time of introspection at the end of the day, reviewing the day's events, your reactions to them, and contemplating how attachment and ego may have played a role. This practice develops self-awareness, a key aspect of letting go, as it helps identify areas where change is needed.

## Mindful Eating

Mindful eating is a practice that fosters a greater connection to and appreciation for the food we consume. It involves eating slowly, savoring each bite, and paying attention to the flavors, textures, and sensations of eating. This practice not only enhances the enjoyment of food but also encourages a deeper appreciation for the nourishment provided, moving away from viewing food merely as an object of desire or indulgence.

## Active Listening

Incorporating active listening into daily interactions is a simple yet effective way to practice letting go of ego. It involves fully focusing on the person speaking, listening without planning your response, and showing genuine interest in their words. This practice fosters deeper, more meaningful connections and helps develop empathy, a key component of humility.

## Nature Connection

Spending time in nature, whether it's a walk in the park, gardening, or simply sitting under a tree, can be a grounding ritual. Nature's inherent simplicity and the cycle of life and decay it demonstrates can be powerful reminders of the principles of non-attachment and impermanence.

## Generosity Acts

Engaging in acts of generosity, whether through volunteer work, helping a neighbor, or simply offering a kind word to a stranger, can reinforce the practice of letting go. These acts of giving, done without expectation of return, cultivate a sense of connectedness and compassion.

## Simplification Rituals

Incorporate rituals of simplification into your life. This might include decluttering your living space, simplifying your wardrobe, or streamlining your daily routines. These actions create physical and mental and emotional space, reducing the clutter of possessions and commitments that often drive attachment.

## Setting Intentions

Begin each day by setting intentions. These intentions should align with the values of non-attachment and humility. It could be as simple as, "Today, I intend to find joy in simple pleasures," or, "Today, I will let go of the need to control outcomes." Setting intentions provides focus and direction for the day.

## Body Scan Meditation

Before sleeping, engage in a body scan meditation. Lie comfortably and slowly bring attention to each part of your body, from your toes to your head. This practice not only relaxes the body but also the mind, helping to release the physical and mental tensions of the day.

## Practicing Forgiveness

Make forgiveness a daily practice. Reflect on any grievances or annoyances and consciously work towards letting them go. This could involve forgiving others or oneself. Forgiveness is a key aspect of letting go and moving forward.

## Learning and Growing

Embrace learning as a daily ritual. This could involve reading, listening to educational podcasts, or engaging in conversations that challenge your perspectives. Continuous learning fosters humility and keeps the mind open and flexible.

## Creating Art

Engage in some form of creative expression regularly, whether it's drawing, writing, music, or dance. Creative activities provide an outlet for emotions and thoughts, facilitating letting go.

Practising these exercises and rituals daily can gradually transform one's approach to life, aligning it more closely with the principles of non-attachment and humility. It's a journey that requires commitment and patience as old habits and thought patterns are replaced with new, more fulfilling ones. Over time, these practices become ingrained, as actions we perform and as integral parts of who we are and how we experience the world. They pave the way to a life characterized by greater peace, deeper connections, and a profound sense of fulfilment that comes from within, independent of external circumstances or possessions.

# *Chapter 10: The Ongoing Journey of Letting Go*

As we reflect on the profound journey explored in this book, it becomes evident that letting go is not just a temporary fix or a one-time effort. It is a continuous, life-long practice that deeply enriches and transforms our lives. This article aims to encapsulate the key insights and lessons gleaned from our exploration, reaffirming the importance of viewing letting go as an integral part of our daily existence. It also seeks to inspire readers with thoughts and quotes highlighting the peace and fulfilment inherent in this spiritual journey.

The core premise of this book revolves around the transformative power of letting go. As we have uncovered, letting go involves more than merely relinquishing physical possessions or superficial desires. It is an internal process of releasing our grip on all that binds us – be it material attachments, ego-driven pursuits, resentments, or rigid beliefs. This practice is about finding freedom, not acquiring more, but appreciating and valuing less.

Much of our journey has been dedicated to understanding how attachment and ego hinder inner peace and fulfilment . We've learned that attachment, while a natural human tendency, can lead to suffering if it morphs into possessiveness or dependency. With its constant need for affirmation and fear of insignificance, the ego often hinders our ability to experience life authentically and fully. Recognizing and addressing these aspects of ourselves is crucial in cultivating a life of true contentment.

Throughout the book, we have emphasized the crucial roles of mindfulness and meditation. These practices offer a pathway to greater self-awareness and peace. By fostering a state of present-moment awareness, we learn to navigate our thoughts and emotions with greater clarity and stability. Meditation, in its various forms, provides a space for introspection and connection with our deeper selves, allowing us to detach from the chaos of the external world.

We have also delved into the application of non-attachment in our relationships and our approach to possessions. In relationships, letting go does not mean detachment or indifference; rather, it's about loving freely without needing control or ownership. Regarding possessions, we have discussed how a life of simplicity and mindfulness can lead to greater joy and less dependency on material comforts for happiness.

A pivotal lesson has been the role of forgiveness and understanding in letting go. Forgiveness allows us to release the past and its associated pain, opening up avenues for healing and growth. Understanding, mainly through empathy, enables us to see situations from different perspectives, fostering compassion and deeper connections.

This journey is not devoid of challenges. It requires a reevaluation of deeply ingrained beliefs and societal norms. It asks for courage to face the unknown and the strength to let go of familiar but unhelpful patterns. However, the rewards of this path are immeasurable. It leads to a life of authenticity, peace, and deeper fulfilment. It cultivates resilience, adaptability, and a profound sense of freedom.

The book has offered various daily practices and rituals to make letting go a consistent part of our lives. These practices range from mindfulness exercises and gratitude journaling to acts of kindness and simplifying our lifestyle. Integrating these practices into our daily routine reinforces our commitment to this path and supports our spiritual growth.

One of the most important takeaways is the understanding that letting go is not a destination but a journey – a continuous learning, growing, and evolving process. It is a practice that we refine and deepen over our lifetime. Embracing letting go as a daily practice ensures that it becomes an integral part of our existence, guiding us towards greater peace and fulfilment.

As we continue on this path, let us draw inspiration from the wisdom of those who have walked this journey before us:

1. "The root of suffering is attachment." – Buddha

2. "You only lose what you cling to." – Siddhārtha Gautama

3. "Letting go means to come to the realization that some people are a part of your history, but not a part of your destiny." – Steve Maraboli

4. "The more you let go, the higher you rise." – Yasmin Mogahed

5. "Simplicity, patience, compassion. These three are your greatest treasures." – Lao Tzu

These thoughts and quotes remind us of the timeless wisdom that underpins the practice of letting go. They encourage us to persevere on this path, reassured that the journey itself is enriching and transformative.

In embracing the ongoing journey of letting go, we open ourselves to a world of infinite possibilities. We learn to live with a lighter heart, a clearer mind, and a deeper connection with the world around us. Let us carry forward this spirit of openness and growth, finding in each moment an opportunity to practice letting go, deepen our understanding, and experience the profound peace and fulfilment this spiritual journey offers. Though filled with challenges, this path is also replete with moments of beauty, joy, and profound realizations – a journey well worth undertaking, with endless opportunities for discovery and transformation.

# About the Author

**Evangeline Brooks**, renowned for her contemplative and insightful approach to life's profound questions, continues her literary journey with her third book, adding another compelling work to her repertoire. Following the success of her earlier works, "The Art of Being Happy: A Philosophical Exploration" and "Meditation and the Path to Self-Discovery: Connecting with Your True Essence," Brooks delves deeper into the realms of personal growth and spirituality. Her latest book builds upon her rich understanding of meditation and philosophy, intertwining practical wisdom with diverse cultural insights. Known for her transformative writing, Brooks offers readers knowledge and a pathway to self-realization and inner peace. Her work is a guiding light for those seeking authenticity and fulfilment in today's complex world.